30 PROPHECIES: ONE STORY

How God's Word points to Jesus

Paul Reynolds

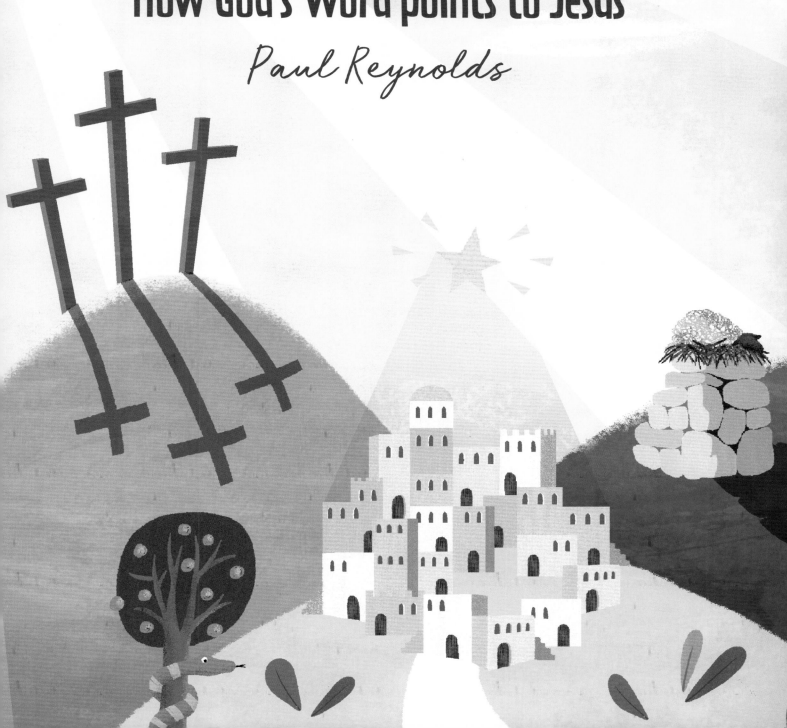

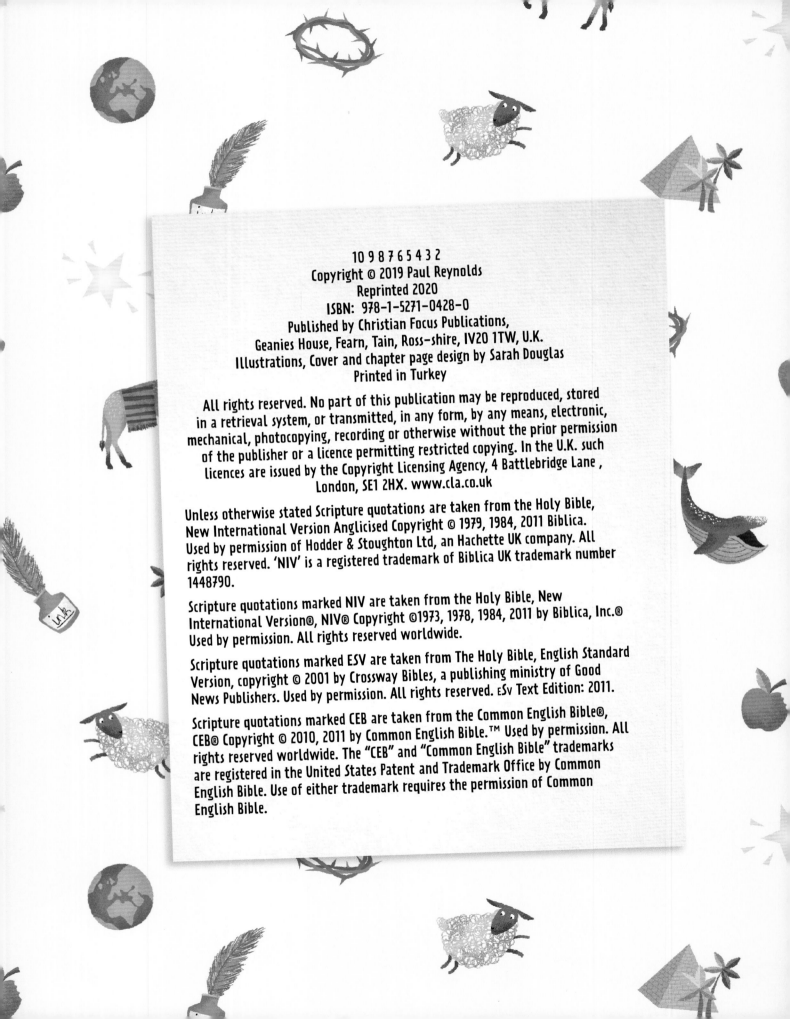

10 9 8 7 6 5 4 3 2
Copyright © 2019 Paul Reynolds
Reprinted 2020
ISBN: 978-1-5271-0428-0
Published by Christian Focus Publications,
Geanies House, Fearn, Tain, Ross-shire, IV20 1TW, U.K.
Illustrations, Cover and chapter page design by Sarah Douglas
Printed in Turkey

DEDICATION

For my wife Rachael, around whom I orbit,
and without whom little of what I do would be
done, and most of it would be worse.

CONTENTS

PROPHECIES MADE BY JESUS ABOUT HIMSELF

INTRODUCTION

On a Sunday afternoon about 2,000 years ago, Cleopas and his friend were making the seven-mile walk from Jerusalem to a town called Emmaus. A very ordinary-looking man joined them and asked what they were talking about. It seemed like a strange question as one event had dominated most people's conversations that weekend: Friday's execution of the very popular Jesus, son of Joseph from Nazareth.

They were very sad, they said, because this man was so good, so powerful and so obviously sent by God that they thought he was going to do amazing things for the Jewish people. The fact that Jesus' body was now reported missing just added to their sadness, as if their grief and sense of loss was now being insulted by grave-thieves.

But their fellow traveller was not as clueless as they first thought. When they told him how sad they were, the first thing he did was call them 'foolish' because they didn't understand that all this was supposed to happen to the Messiah but that it would end well.

'And beginning with Moses and all the Prophets, he explained to them what was said in all the Scriptures concerning himself'[1]. You see, their fellow-traveller wasn't just a random guy – he was Jesus himself, but they didn't realise until later on that evening.

This book will take us into that conversation Jesus had with Cleopas and his friend and what he was trying to help them understand. We will go on a tour of some of what 'Moses and all the Prophets' said about Jesus. Who were they talking to? What did it mean to those people? How was any of it about Jesus?

Different people have different ideas about how many prophecies in the Old Testament are about Jesus. One suggestion is that there are 353 prophecies regarding the coming of Jesus. I have chosen thirty for the purposes of this book.

My prayer is that as you see the prophecies God inspired his prophets to make, you will see what God has done through Jesus, and you will want to know him.

1. Luke 24:27

12

PROPHET/DATES – WHO WAS GOD'S MESSENGER, TAKING THE PROPHECY TO THE PEOPLE, AND WHEN DID IT HAPPEN?

 PROPHECY MADE & PROPHECY FULFILLED – DIRECT QUOTES FROM THE BIBLE OF THE PROPHECY ITSELF AND ITS FULFILMENT. SOMETIMES THE BIBLE RECORDS MORE THAN ONE EXAMPLE OF THE ORIGINAL OR THE FULFILMENT AND IN THOSE SITUATIONS I'VE QUOTED JUST ONE.

 THEN AND THERE – WHAT THE PROPHECY MEANT TO THE ORIGINAL HEARERS

 PROPHECY FULFILLED – HOW JESUS FULFILS THE PROPHECY

 SCARLET THREAD – HOW DOES THIS PROPHECY FIT IN WITH WHAT GOD IS SAYING ABOUT HIS 'ONE STORY'? THE STORY OF HOW HE IS SAVING PEOPLE FROM SATAN AND KEEPING THEM SAFE TO BE WITH HIM FOREVER?

 APPLICATION – SO YOU'VE LEARNED ABOUT THE PROPHECY, THE FULFILMENT, AND HOW IT TIES IN TO GOD'S ONE STORY ... BUT WHAT DOES THAT MEAN FOR YOU?

 PRAYER – THERE ARE MANY THINGS YOU COULD PRAY ABOUT AFTER LEARNING ABOUT ONE OF THESE PROPHECIES. THE PRAYER GIVEN IS AN EXAMPLE OF SOMETHING YOU COULD PRAY IN RESPONSE TO WHAT YOU HAVE JUST LEARNED OR BEEN REMINDED OF.

PROPHECY TIMELINE

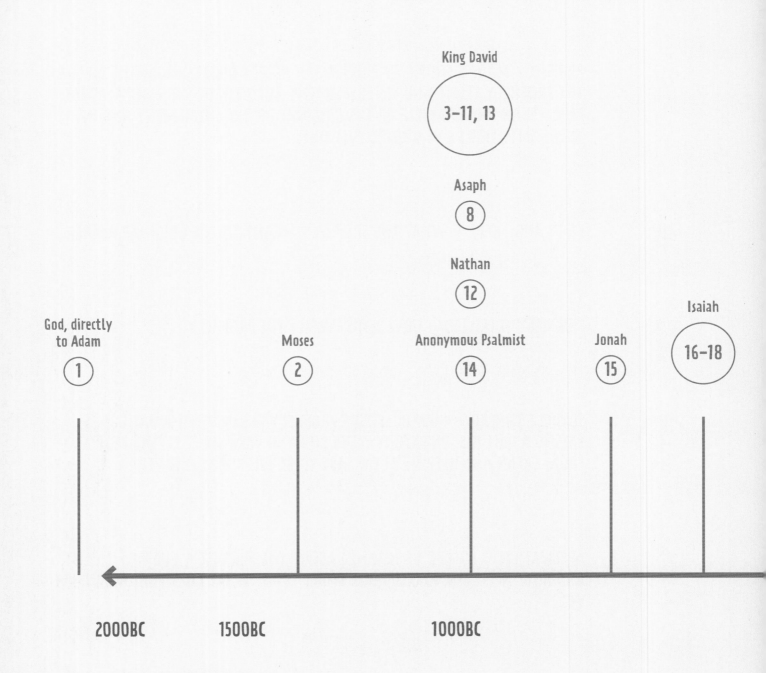

Words: These are the biblical authors.

Circled Numbers: These refer to the chapters in the book.

Timeline scale varies.

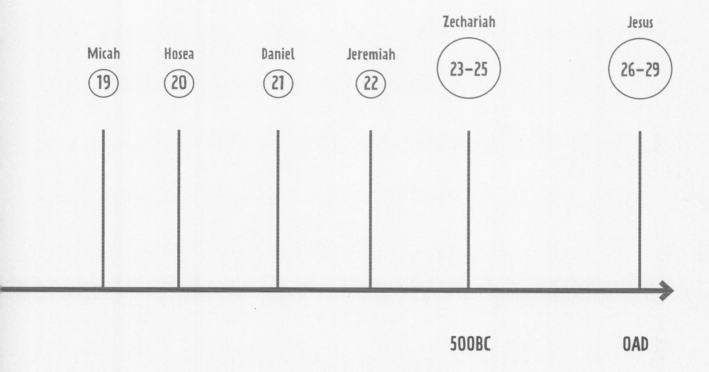

Micah
(19)

Hosea
(20)

Daniel
(21)

Jeremiah
(22)

Zechariah
23–25

Jesus
26–29

500BC

0AD

FROM THE FALL
TO KING DAVID

JESUS: HE DEFEATED THE DEVIL'S WORK

MAY 22

PROPHET/DATES: God, directly to Adam and Eve after the first sin. Date unknown.

PROPHECY MADE: God said to the snake, 'And I will put enmity between you and the woman, and between your offspring and hers; he will crush your head, and you will strike his heel' (Genesis 3:15).

THEN AND THERE: The best news in history came right after the worst thing that ever happened. Evil entered the world for the first time when Adam and Eve ate the fruit that God told them not to eat, after Satan tempted them. God's promise to defeat Satan and evil came right after that.

Satan is symbolised by the snake, and all people are represented by 'the woman' (Eve). When it talks about the 'offspring' of 'the woman' it's mainly talking about all people, but especially Jesus – God himself – who was born of a woman and who, according to this prophecy, would one day crush Satan. It couldn't be talking about an ordinary person because Satan is stronger than all of us. Satan even convinced Adam and Eve

that God was holding back his best from them and they should disobey him. If Satan convinced them of a great nonsense like that, it's no surprise that we so often give in to the lies of temptation.

However, God in his great mercy didn't wait around and leave Adam and Eve thinking that no good could ever come because of what they had done. Even though their sin brought the curses of death and pain into the world, God would one day provide someone who would completely defeat Satan. However, Satan would cause great pain to people and even to the promised 'offspring' – the 'great somebody' who would defeat Satan.

PROPHECY FULFILLED: '… the devil has been sinning from the beginning. The reason the Son of God appeared was to destroy the devil's work' (1 John 3:8).

See also: 'Since the children have flesh and blood, he too shared in their humanity so that by his death he might break the power of him who holds the power of death – that is, the devil' (Hebrews 2:14).

SCARLET THREAD: We now know the name of that great promised 'somebody': Jesus. He was the only person ever born who could defeat Satan completely because although Jesus came to earth as a man, he is still also God.

Why do you think that Jesus came to earth? What was he hoping to do or to achieve? This verse tells us: 'to destroy the devil's work'. The devil's work is to get as many people to suffer as much as possible, and he does that mainly by trying to keep people away from God; away from forgiveness, away from knowing Jesus, away from having joy in their lives.

God promised through the prophets that he would send someone to take the punishment for our sins, because that is the only way we could be saved and be able to have a good relationship with God.

APPLICATION: Thank God that he kept his promise to send someone – born of a woman – who would 'crush Satan's head' to destroy his work. Thank God for Jesus.

Did you know that God is stronger than the devil? Jesus has already destroyed the devil's big plan to keep everyone away from God, and when Jesus comes again the devil won't be able to do *anything* to *anyone* any more.

PRAYER: God, thank you that through Jesus' perfect life, his death and being raised again to life, that the devil's work has been destroyed and anyone can have free forgiveness of their sins. Please help everyone to know that. Amen.

JESUS: A PROPHET LIKE MOSES

MAY
22

PROPHET/DATES: Moses, 1400 BC – God's instructions to Moses about living in the Promised Land.

PROPHECY MADE: 'I will raise up for them a prophet like you from among their fellow Israelites, and I will put my words in his mouth. He will tell them everything I command him. I myself will call to account anyone who does not listen to my words that the prophet speaks in my name' (Deuteronomy 18:18-19).

THEN AND THERE: The Israelites were in the desert during their forty years of wandering when God gave Moses a lot of instructions about how the people should live when they finally arrived in the Promised Land and made it their home. God told them that they needed to obey him. They were not to be like all the people around them.

God promised through Moses that he would send a prophet who would speak God's exact words to the people. It was crucial for them to listen to him and obey him.

Over the next 1,000 years God spoke to his people mainly through angels and prophets. The people could tell who the real prophets were because when they predicted the future, it came true. When they made a prediction that didn't come true … well, then the people knew they were dealing with a false prophet who was not from God. Also, many of God's prophets performed miracles, which proved God was with them.

Many of the prophecies were important messages from God for the people then and there. Sadly and often, the people refused to listen and God had to punish them for it, until one day God sent the ultimate prophet – the only person in history who always spoke the perfect words of God. That man was Jesus.

PROPHECY FULFILLED: 'For Moses said, "The Lord your God will raise up for you a prophet like me from among your own people; you must listen to everything he tells you. Anyone who does not listen to him will be completely cut off from their people"' (Acts 3:22-23).

'After the people saw the sign Jesus performed, they began to say, "Surely this is the Prophet who is to come into the world." Jesus, knowing that they intended to come and make him king by force, withdrew again to a mountain by himself' (John 6:14-15).

SCARLET THREAD: God's people had been waiting, not just for a prophet like Moses, but *the* prophet like Moses. When Jesus came a lot of people began to wonder. 'Is this the guy?' Part of the way through Jesus' ministry people thought maybe he was, but most had the wrong idea of what to do about it. Jesus did not come to rule over them like an earthly king – he came to save them from their sins. Sometimes Jesus had to just go away into the countryside on his own so they couldn't force him to become king.

Can you imagine anyone wanting to force you to rule over them? No, me neither. But that's what they wanted to do to Jesus.

The apostle Peter was thinking about this on the day of Pentecost when he was talking to the crowds about who Jesus was. He was trying to help them understand that all the prophecies they read about in the Bible came true in Jesus. Even this *really* ancient prophecy from nearly 1,500 years earlier, which came through Moses.

Peter said this because he wanted to remind the people about the last bit of the prophecy: that people *must* listen to what *the* prophet said so that they could be saved from their sins by trusting in Jesus.

APPLICATION: If you went to the doctor and they took your temperature, you would listen very carefully to what they said next because you know that they know more than you about bodies and illnesses. For example, if they said you had an infection and needed to take some medicine, you would do as they told you.

Jesus knows more than you, me, and everyone else about how to be in a right relationship with God the Father, so we must listen carefully to what he says and do what he says. How do we know? Because God the Father himself tells us so in these verses. And the most important two things that Jesus says we must do is to say sorry to God for being a sinner and ask him for forgiveness.

Do you 'listen' to what Jesus says by reading about it in the Bible, and then obeying it? Do you trust Jesus as much as you trust your doctor?

PRAYER: God, thank you that the prophecy through Moses came true in Jesus. Please help me to obey what Jesus said, to ask you to forgive my sins, and to be really sorry for my sin. Amen.

JESUS: A PRIEST LIKE MELCHIZEDEK

MAY
22

PROPHET/DATES: King David, around 1000 BC.

PROPHECY MADE: 'The LORD has sworn and will not change his mind: "You are a priest for ever, in the order of Melchizedek"' (Psalm 110:4).

THEN AND THERE: The psalms were mainly songs of sadness, worry, praise, thanks or happiness. The psalm writers were usually creating poetry rather than prophecy, but when King David wrote Psalm 110 he was giving people – in poetry form – a prophecy direct from God.

King David may have been talking, in the first instance, about his son, Solomon, who would become king before David died. Usually the son of the king only took over once the king was dead, but Solomon became king while David was still alive, when David handed the kingdom over to him and knew that God would be with him. Melchizedek was a famous king from Abraham's time, who was also a priest. He was very highly respected, so when David compared his son to Melchizedek he was saying his son would be important to the people and that God would be greatly respected.

PROPHECY FULFILLED: 'In the same way, Christ did not take on himself the glory of becoming a high priest. But God said to him, "You are my Son; today I have become your Father." And he says in another place, "You are a priest for ever, in the order of Melchizedek"… Without father or mother, without genealogy, without beginning of days or end of life, resembling the Son of God, he remains a priest forever' (Hebrews 5:5-6; 7:3).

SCARLET THREAD: This psalm is not just about David and Solomon. Psalm 110 is also a prophetic message from God the Father to God the Son, telling him about the glories and victories that are coming to him, including the defeat of all his enemies. The Jews knew – even in Old Testament times – that this was talking about the Messiah.

Jesus was the great High Priest; he offered the sacrifice to God that would be for the salvation of God's people, as well as being the sacrifice itself! At the same time he was and is the King of all those who put their trust in God to have their sins forgiven. In the Old Testament, only one person had ever been King and High Priest, and that man was Melchizedek; he and Jesus are linked by having both those titles.

Melchizedek didn't literally live forever on earth and have no parents, but we don't hear of his birth or death, or his parents or children, so the writer of Hebrews links him to Jesus. Melchizedek was a 'type' of Jesus, like some other Old Testament figures such as King David. That means Melchizedek had things in common with Jesus about who he was and what he did. Melchizedek is used by God to help us understand more things about Jesus.

The most important way that Melchizedek and Jesus are linked is that both of them were priests, and not from the tribe of Levi as was required of all other priests but superior to them. Melchizedek was a priest before Levi was born, and Jesus is a priest forever.

APPLICATION: When people make promises there are at least two things that can go wrong. First, they might change their mind later and decide to go against their promise. Or they might not be able to keep their promise even though they try.

We know God is able to keep his promises and in this verse he reminds us that he will, because there is no chance he would change his mind. Wouldn't it be great if people were like that! Sadly we are not, but it is wonderful to know that God is.

Jesus made the once-and-for-all sacrifice so that no more need to be offered. If we are trusting him for the forgiveness of our sin, Jesus is still our High Priest. His sacrifice means we are still forgiven, and he is still representing us to his Father in heaven – asking the Father to help us and to forgive our sin.

PRAYER: Thank you, God, that Jesus is a King forever and our Great High Priest, ruling in heaven and talking to you for us. Amen.

④

JESUS: REJECTED BY HIS BROTHERS

MAY 22

PROPHET/DATES: King David, around 1000 BC.

PROPHECY MADE: 'I have become a stranger to my brothers, an alien to my mother's sons' (Psalm 69:8 ESV).

THEN AND THERE: King David was in a terrible situation. Many times in his life people tried to kill him, or take over the country, or take over as king and this was one of those times.

Earlier in the psalm, David said he felt like he was drowning. This means that things were so awful he felt helpless, that however much he tried to fix the situation, everything just got worse. It felt as though he was so deep in water that he was starting to go under the water. In this verse he is saying that not only are his enemies against him (which he expected and was prepared for), but he had been abandoned even by those closest to him – his own brothers. That might have been a reference mainly to his 'brother' Jews – that is, his fellow-countrymen whom he had served as king, and not just his siblings.

Do you know what it feels like when people are against you or are being mean to you? It can make a huge difference when you have your family or friends to back you up, to give you comfort, or defend you. But imagine if those people who were supposed to defend you just abandoned you. You would feel terribly alone and the meanness of other people would feel worse.

PROPHECY FULFILLED: 'Jesus' brothers said to him, "Leave Galilee and go to Judea, so that your disciples there may see the works you do. No one who wants to become a public figure acts in secret. Since you are doing these things, show yourself to the world." For even his own brothers did not believe in him' (John 7:3-5).

SCARLET THREAD: Galilee was in the north of the country, where Jesus grew up. It was a mountainous area with not many big towns so if you wanted to be famous you wouldn't stay there long. Especially if your own family didn't support you! It would be a bit like growing up in a village in the desert, or a tiny island that didn't get visitors. If you were from a place like that and people thought you wanted to be famous they might say, 'Hey, you should move to Los Angeles, Paris, or London! You would get many more followers if you lived there!' That must have been so discouraging for Jesus. His own brothers, who'd lived with him all their lives and had never seen him sin, who knew the miracles that he'd done, did not believe that he was God.

His brothers said this soon after a lot of Jesus' disciples had left him (not some of the twelve special disciples – Jesus had many other disciples also[2]).

Jesus knew how King David felt! As well as his brothers not believing in who Jesus was, his disciples didn't understand who he was for three years and one of his best friends – Peter – pretended that he didn't even know Jesus after Jesus got arrested.

We may never know what it feels like to be that lonely and abandoned by those closest to us, but Jesus did and although he could have escaped the bad situation any time he wanted, he stuck with it. Why? Because by sticking with the plan, by obeying his Father, he was loving his Father and loving us because Jesus' obedience means that we can be saved from our sins.

And Jesus didn't just feel rejected by his brothers – he also felt rejection from his own Father while he was on the cross, but we'll read about that in another chapter.

APPLICATION: How would it feel if your own family didn't support you? If they seemed to prefer other people to you or refused to even believe that you were part of the family? King David's brothers did not support him as king, and Jesus' brothers did not believe he was God.

Most parents love their children very much and give up a lot for them, but there is only one person who will always love us perfectly, and that is God. Even if everyone else falls away from us and doesn't support us any more, God will always be there.

So we should stick with Jesus. It doesn't matter how many other people don't seem interested in Jesus any more – we must always stick by him. Not because he needs us to defend him, but because we need him to defend us and stay with us. We must hold onto him like a baby holds onto her parents. Why? Because God does so much for us, loves us more than anyone, and we need him.

PRAYER: God, thank you that Jesus stuck with the plan to love and obey you, and to love us. Thank you that he didn't give up when his own brothers didn't believe in him and gave him bad advice. Please help us to stay with you always and love you, because we know that you will never abandon us. Amen.

---

2. The word 'disciple' just means 'follower'. So everyone who followed Jesus was called a 'disciple'. When we use the word we are usually referring to one of the twelve special disciples that Jesus told to follow him, and who were his close friends.
* The picture opposite shows King David being pursued by his enemies. Throughout the book David is portrayed by the artist in the same kind of clothes in each illustration: a striped tunic, sometimes with a crown. Look at pages 24, 28, 30, 34, 38, 42, 44.

⑤

JESUS: HIS BONES WERE NOT BROKEN

MAY 22

PROPHET/DATES: King David, around 1000 BC.

PROPHECY MADE: 'The righteous person may have many troubles, but the LORD delivers him from them all; he protects all his bones, not one of them will be broken' (Psalm 34:19-20).

"[The Passover lamb] must be eaten inside the house; take none of the meat outside the house. Do not break any of the bones" (Exodus 12:46).

THEN AND THERE: King Saul of Israel wanted to kill David the shepherd boy, even though David had done nothing wrong and didn't want to hurt Saul. David ran away to Gath (one of Israel's enemies) and pretended to be mad in the hope that King Abimelech of Gath would just leave him alone. That worked for a while but then they told him he had to go. So, because nowhere was safe for him to be seen, he went and hid out in a cave.

This psalm was written while David was in Gath. What would you write a song about if your own king was trying to kill you and you were staying with your enemy pretending to be mad so that he didn't kill you? Maybe you would be angry, or sad, or depressed, or lonely, or scared, or full of worry. Probably you would be a little bit of all those things.

It is amazing that the first line of this psalm is David saying that he will praise God at all times. He then tells people how great God is, and how he protects and saves his people. David obviously had a great amount of trust in God even at the very worst time.

This section of the psalm is David reminding people that no matter how bad things get, God is always there to rescue them. In the Old Testament when God's people were obeying him he didn't let their enemies defeat them. Throughout David's life God rescued him or the Israelites during wars and other difficulties, so when he said that God protects his people, he knew what he was talking about! If the people only knew one story about David before he was king, it would have been how young David defeated the giant Goliath with only a sling and a stone from the river.

When David wrote about no bones getting broken, the people would have understood that as being picture language describing how God's protection is perfect.

The Exodus verse is from God's instructions to his people for the festival of the Passover when God rescued them from Egypt. It adds to the picture that God is building for his people of the perfect sacrifice – the animal to be used had to be one that had nothing wrong with it at all, like a bad eye, or a limp.

PROPHECY FULFILLED: 'But when they came to Jesus and found that he was already dead, they did not break his legs. Instead, one of the soldiers pierced Jesus' side with a spear, bringing a sudden flow of blood and water. The man who saw it has given testimony, and his testimony is true. He knows that he tells the truth, and he testifies so that you also may believe. These things happened so that the scripture would be fulfilled: "Not one of his bones will be broken ..."' (John 19:33-36).

SCARLET THREAD: God had been building the picture in the Old Testament of the need for a perfect sacrifice. Then he sent that perfect sacrifice: Jesus. Jesus was God on earth, perfect in every way, completely without sin. Before Jesus was killed, the soldiers beat and did other awful things to him, but no bones were broken. The criminals crucified with him had their legs broken to make them die sooner, but because Jesus was already dead, they left his legs alone. The prophecy was coming true in every way. It seems like such a little detail, but it gives us an important lesson about the perfection of Jesus.

APPLICATION: What's the most scary situation you have been in? When I was a teenager I was stuck down a cave with a group of friends. What made it worse was that it was my fault because I was the leader! It got so bad that I was thinking, I might get injured by these big rocks, but I'm going to have to do *something* to get us out. Fortunately that wasn't necessary because someone came to rescue us – thank God, no-one was hurt!

The biggest trouble we can have is from Satan who wants to take people away from God, but God will never let that happen to his people.[3] In the Old Testament God showed his love with promises to protect his people from their enemies on earth. God shows his love now with promises to protect us from Satan if we repent and put our trust in God.

PRAYER: Thank you, God, that you kept your promise to provide a perfect sacrifice for sin. Help us to trust you that you have done all the work so that we can have free forgiveness. Help us to remember that you will always protect your people, no matter what. Amen.

---

3. 'For I am convinced that neither death nor life, neither angels nor demons, neither the present nor the future, nor any powers, neither height nor depth, nor anything else in all creation, will be able to separate us from the love of God that is in Christ Jesus our Lord' (Romans 8:38-39).

JESUS: REJECTED BY HIS FATHER

PROPHET/DATES: King David, around 1000 BC.

PROPHECY MADE: 'My God, my God, why have you forsaken me? Why are you so far from saving me, so far from my cries of anguish? My God, I cry out by day, but you do not answer, by night, but I find no rest. Yet you are enthroned as the Holy One; you are the one Israel praises' (Psalm 22:1-3).

THEN AND THERE: This psalm has a lot of prophecy about Jesus and was written 1,000 years before he was on earth. David went through terrible situations in his life including fear and danger. He was hunted, people hated him, and people he loved died. When he was king his own son brought an army to fight against him and David was forced to run away.

In this psalm he is going through one of those awful times. It was so bad that he felt God no longer cared about him and had gone away from him, ignoring his prayers

and cries for help. He felt like he could go through anything if God was with him, and didn't understand why God seemed to have gone away.

At the end of these verses David had hope again. Try reading the rest of the psalm – David got more and more filled with hope in God. He remembered that God is praised by his people because of how loving and fair and powerful he is. David remembered that God rules over all things and listens to the shouts and crying of those who are suffering. And God always does the best thing.

PROPHECY FULFILLED: 'Going a little farther, he fell with his face to the ground and prayed, "My Father, if it is possible, may this cup be taken from me. Yet not as I will, but as you will"' (Matthew 26:39).

'From noon until three in the afternoon darkness came over all the land. About three in the afternoon Jesus cried out in a loud voice, "Eli, Eli, lema sabachthani?" (which means, "My God, my God, why have you forsaken me?")' (Matthew 27:45-46).

SCARLET THREAD: The prophecy was partially fulfilled while Jesus was praying in the Garden of Gethsemane – just before Judas Iscariot betrayed him. Jesus knew that he was going to have to go through incredible suffering and asked God to remove the suffering from him. But he did have to go through it, because it was through his suffering. He was punished instead of sinful people like you and me – that our sins can be forgiven.

Jesus prayed for hours and God sent an angel to comfort him, while Jesus was thinking about the terrible things that were going to happen to him.

During Jesus' suffering he felt much worse than David, and while he was on the cross he used the exact same words as David. He also felt that God the Father had left him, and with his words he showed that what David said was not only about David. It was more a prophecy about Jesus himself. Jesus' physical suffering was terrible, but even worse was the fact that he became separated in his relationship with his Father God. That relationship had been perfect from eternity to that point and now suddenly God the Father had left Jesus because Jesus was carrying our sinfulness.

Jesus' feeling of being rejected by his Father was completely strange to him – different and the opposite from everything he had experienced up to that point. It was worse than anything you can imagine. But he did it out of love, to save people from their sins. Like David, Jesus knew that his Father would not leave him forever. We know that because, even though Jesus died, he was later raised from the dead.

APPLICATION: We all want to feel that when we pray, God is listening. But of course, we don't just want him to listen, we want him to say 'Yes!' every time we ask him for something, or ask him to stop something. If he even said 'No' to Jesus, he'll definitely say 'No' to us sometimes. The 'No' to Jesus gives us a great example of how God is still full of love when he says that, and how he will still do everything perfectly, just as he did back then.

PRAYER: Thank you, God, that we can praise you as our perfect, holy, powerful, loving and protecting God, even when we can't always feel that you are with us. Thank you that Jesus trusted and loved you enough, and loved us enough, to go through with all that suffering so that we can be saved. Thank you that he didn't give up. Please help us to always trust and love you. Amen.

JESUS: MOCKED AND CHALLENGED

MAY
22

PROPHET/DATES: King David, around 1000 BC.

PROPHECY MADE: 'But I am a worm and not a man, scorned by everyone, despised by the people. All who see me mock me; they hurl insults, shaking their heads. "He trusts in the LORD," they say, "let the LORD rescue him. Let him deliver him, since he delights in him"' (Psalm 22:6-8).

THEN AND THERE: David didn't think he was literally a worm. He was saying that is the way we might think about worms: tiny, useless[4], easily squished … that's the way that people were thinking about him and it was the way he was beginning to think about himself.

This is our second look at King David's words in Psalm 22 as he struggled against his enemies and his own feelings of rejection. When David's son Absalom was publicly disrespecting his father and everyone seemed to be taking Absalom's side, David began to look weak and vulnerable and some people who had supported David went to

---

4. They're actually very useful – the tunnels they make help air and water get to the roots of plants, helping them to grow.

support his son instead. Even as David was running away, a man called Shimei cursed David as a murderer and said he deserved all the bad things that were happening to him.

The picture in these verses is one of God's people suffering, being made fun of and thought stupid by people who have no love for God.

PROPHECY FULFILLED: 'Those who passed by hurled insults at [Jesus], shaking their heads and saying, "You who are going to destroy the temple and build it in three days, save yourself! Come down from the cross, if you are the Son of God!" In the same way the chief priests, the teachers of the law and the elders mocked him. "He saved others," they said, "but he can't save himself! He's the king of Israel! Let him come down now from the cross, and we will believe in him. He trusts in God. Let God rescue him now if he wants him, for he said, 'I am the Son of God.'" In the same way the rebels who were crucified with him also heaped insults on him' (Matthew 27:39-44).

SCARLET THREAD: All sorts of people were laughing at Jesus and making fun of him while he was on the cross, because they thought he was helpless. Jesus had prophesied saying that *they* could destroy the temple and he would raise it again in three days; they were wrong in saying that Jesus said *he* would destroy it. They got their facts wrong about what he said and didn't understand that he was talking about his resurrection, so all they could think of to do was insult him while he was dying.

When the religious leaders said 'He's the King of Israel!' they didn't believe it. They were talking about the sign over Jesus' head written by the Roman governor which said that's what he was. We don't know exactly what they thought but it was their hatred and jealousy of Jesus that meant he was being killed, even though he was innocent.

That's the kind of person who makes fun of God: someone who either doesn't even believe God exists, or doesn't know who they're dealing with. Making fun of God doesn't make any sense, because God has all the power, but he's also a God of love who doesn't want anyone to come to harm.

When the religious leaders told Jesus to come down off the cross to prove he was the true King of Israel and the world, that must have been a temptation to Jesus because he *could* have come down off the cross if he'd wanted to. The only reason he didn't is because he was determined to obey his Father God, and save people from their sins. His desire to love and serve his Father was greater than his desire to avoid great pain. And remember, God the Father *did* deliver Jesus from death – he rose again!

APPLICATION: Do people ever make fun of you for what you think or what you believe? This often happens when someone has an opinion or a faith that is different to the main group. It feels horrible, doesn't it? Satan wanted King David, and he wanted Jesus to feel that God had abandoned them. Satan wants you to feel that people are being mean to you and that God has abandoned you. But the stories of King David and Jesus show that, just like everything else Satan says, that's a lie. God never abandons his people and he stays with them forever. If people make fun of you or are mean to you because you believe in God, or go to church, or read the Bible, tell Jesus about it. He knows how you feel and has had the same and much worse things done to him.

PRAYER: God, thank you that Jesus died to save us from our sins, and thank you that you raised him from the dead to be with you again forever in heaven. Please help me to love you even when people are nasty to me about it, and help me to remember that if I am with you, you will never leave me. Amen.

JESUS: SPOKE IN PARABLES

MAY 22

PROPHET/DATES: Asaph, around 1000 BC.

PROPHECY MADE: 'I will open my mouth with a parable, I will utter hidden things, things from of old …' (Psalm 78:2).

THEN AND THERE: Asaph from the tribe of Levi was King David's director of music at the temple[5]. He wrote twelve psalms that are in the Bible, including this one: number 78. He may also have written the music to some of the psalms by King David.

This psalm reminded the people about everything God had done for them in the past (e.g. rescuing them from slavery in Egypt, bringing them into the Promised Land of Canaan, defeating their enemies in battle). Asaph also reminded them of their sin and God's holiness as a warning for them to obey him, and talked about God's great patience and love for them.

When Asaph said, 'I will open my mouth with a parable,' he didn't know that he was prophesying, although he knew that he was a prophet[6].

---

5. 1 Chronicles 16:4-5
6. 1 Chronicles 25:1

PROPHECY FULFILLED: 'Jesus spoke all these things to the crowd in parables; he did not say anything to them without using a parable. So was fulfilled what was spoken through the prophet: "I will open my mouth in parables, I will utter things hidden since the creation of the world"' (Matthew 13:34-35).

 SCARLET THREAD: Jesus often taught in parables: simple stories with one main lesson. He had just got through telling the Parable of the Sower, the Parable of the Weeds and the Parable of the Mustard Seed and Yeast. He had also told them that by speaking the truth in parables many people (those who were rejecting him) would not understand what he was saying to them.

In the Parable of the Sower he taught about how people responded to the Word of God. He likened God telling people about himself to a sower throwing seed on the ground. Some of that seed fell on good soil where it grew up into a healthy crop – that was like people who heard God's Word, understood it and acted on it by repenting and turning to Jesus.

But other seed fell on different types of bad soil, for example some fell among weeds so that the wheat grew quickly, but then got choked by the weeds and died. That is like people who listen to God's Word but quickly get distracted by things they are worried about and forget about what God has said.

Jesus was talking about things that no one sent by God had spoken about before. He was helping people to understand more about God, about themselves, and about the people around them.

 APPLICATION: When you read the Bible or you hear about what Jesus said, what kind of seed are you like? Do you respond to and obey what Jesus said, like the seed that grew up into healthy plants? Or do you get distracted, or worried, or more interested in other things? Don't worry about what you have been in the past, but ask God now to help you.

 PRAYER: God, thank you that Jesus taught the people many things 2,000 years ago that are all still true today. Please help me not just to hear what God says in the Bible but to do something about it as well. And please help me to understand what the Bible says so that I can know you better. Amen.

⑨

JESUS: BETRAYED BY A FRIEND

MAY 22

PROPHET/DATES: King David, around 1000 BC.

PROPHECY MADE: 'All my enemies whisper together against me; they imagine the worst for me … Even my close friend, someone I trusted, one who shared my bread, has turned against me' (Psalm 41:7-9).

THEN AND THERE: King David was sick – so sick that many people thought he would die. David was convinced that it was happening to him as a punishment from God – he says so in the psalm when he asks God to have mercy on him, because David has sinned against God.

However, even though he had sinned – and David did some big sins in his life – David loved and trusted God, and wanted to do what was right. In this parable he was asking

GUESS WHAT?!

34

God to heal him so that he could get revenge on the people who were plotting against him, hoping he died. The worst thing for David wasn't that his enemies wanted him dead; he was used to that. Rather, what hurt him the most was that even one of his close friends became one of his enemies, turning against him.

David may have been talking about his army commander Joab (a wicked man), his son Absalom or even someone we don't read about in the Bible. We don't know, the point is to understand how terrible David felt.

PROPHECY FULFILLED: 'When evening came, Jesus was reclining at the table with the Twelve. And while they were eating, he said, "Truly I tell you, one of you will betray me."

They were very sad and began to say to him one after the other, "Surely you don't mean me, Lord?"

Jesus replied, "The one who has dipped his hand into the bowl with me will betray me. The Son of Man will go just as it is written about him. But woe to that man who betrays the Son of Man! It would be better for him if he had not been born."

Then Judas, the one who would betray him, said, "Surely you don't mean me, Rabbi?"

Jesus answered, "You have said so [yourself]"' (Matthew 26:20-25).

SCARLET THREAD: The religious leaders had been plotting for years, trying to find a way to get Jesus killed. It was hard because they didn't always know where Jesus was going to be and they were afraid of the people, many of whom thought Jesus was amazing and probably sent by God. Then along came Judas Iscariot – one of Jesus' closest friends, who knew where Jesus was going to be. Judas told them how they could arrest Jesus at night, in the dark, without the crowds around to protest about it or stop them.

Jesus was eating dinner with his disciples to celebrate the festival of the Passover, remembering how God had rescued his people from slavery in Egypt 1,500 years earlier. On the first Passover day, a lamb was sacrificed and the blood smeared on the door frames of the Israelites' houses. Then, when the angel of death passed by, killing the firstborn in every household, the houses with the blood on the door frames were spared the tragedy. The lambs died so that all the people could live.

Here was Jesus – the Lamb of God – getting ready to be the sacrifice so that God's people could live. And as if that wasn't enough, the way it would happen was going to fulfil the prophecy made by King David, that Jesus would be betrayed by a friend: Judas Iscariot, who ate with Jesus.

Making his prophecy even more clear, Jesus gave Judas Iscariot a piece of bread, confirmed that yes, he was the betrayer, and told Judas to get on and do what he was going to do[7]. Perhaps the saddest thing in this is Judas Iscariot himself. We don't know why he asked whether he was the betrayer – perhaps he hoped Jesus wouldn't know – but here he had one final chance to change his mind. He had one final opportunity, confronted by his friend and guide Jesus, to say, 'No, even if the Pharisees make me rich, I still don't want to betray the chosen one of God, my friend.' But he didn't do that. He went ahead and did exactly what he planned to do, betraying his friend.

7. John 13:21 & 26 'After he had said this, Jesus was troubled in spirit and testified, "Very truly I tell you, one of you is going to betray me" ... It is the one to whom I will give this piece of bread when I have dipped it in the dish." Then, dipping the piece of bread, he gave it to Judas, the son of Simon Iscariot.'

Handing over God himself – betraying him to his enemies to be killed – was the worst thing that anyone has ever done. God used that betrayal to do the most wonderful thing that has ever been done: paying the penalty for people's sins. God can use anything to do what needs to be done, even using wicked people and evil actions like this.

APPLICATION: Do you know what it is like to have one of your friends suddenly turn against you? It happens a lot: to children in schools, grown-ups in offices and many other places. If there is someone who doesn't like you, it isn't a surprise if they say bad things about you to other people, although it still isn't nice. King David had to put up with people fighting against him and people wishing him dead. Jesus had to put up with one of his twelve close friends, with whom he had spent a lot of time in the previous three years, betray him to his enemies just to get a bit of money.

If you had asked Judas Iscariot whether he liked Jesus the answer would most likely have been yes, but in the end money was more important to him than his relationship with Jesus, more important even than Jesus' life.

It is easy for us to say that we love Jesus, but do we show that in the way that we live? For example, when we talk to other people about who our friends are, and what we like doing and what we think about, do we ever tell them about Jesus?

PRAYER: God, thank you that even though Judas Iscariot sinned in the worst sin possible, you used that to make the prophecy come true. It was part of your plan to save your people from their sins. Please help me not to pretend to be your friend like Judas did, but to really love you and show it in the way that I live, the things that I say, and by praying to you and reading the Bible. Amen.

All my enemies whisper together against me.

 Which

I will utter hidden things,
things from of old.

... scorned by everyone, despised by the people ...

My God, my God, why have
you forsaken me?

 psalm

he protects all his bones ...

 is this?

You are a priest for ever, in the order of
Melchizedek.

JESUS: HE DIED
AND ROSE FROM THE DEAD SOON AFTERWARDS

MAY

22

PROPHET/DATES: King David, around 1000 BC.

PROPHECY MADE: '... my heart is glad and my tongue rejoices; my body also will rest secure, because you will not abandon me to the realm of the dead, nor will you let your faithful one see decay' (Psalm 16:9-10).

THEN AND THERE: 'Keep me safe, my God, for in you I take refuge' is the first line of the psalm. King David said that there is no point looking to anyone else for help and protection because it can only come from God, who taught him many things as well as saving him. David knew – even as he asked God for protection – that God's answer was yes, that God would always protect him, never abandon him, never leave him alone, and always be with him.

This psalm would have been very encouraging, reminding people to put their trust in God as the only one we can always trust, who has the love and the power to always take care of his people.

Verse 11 sums up how excited David was to belong to God: 'You make known to me the path of life; you will fill me with joy in your presence, with eternal pleasures at your right hand.'

PROPHECY FULFILLED: 'David died and was buried, and his tomb is here to this day. But he was a prophet and knew that God had promised him on oath that he would place one of his descendants on his throne. Seeing what was to come, he spoke of the resurrection of the Messiah, that he was not abandoned to the grave, nor did his body see decay' (Acts 2:29-31).

SCARLET THREAD: David was talking about himself, his need of protection, and his own joy that God had given him when he wrote that psalm. But he also knew that he was going to die so he wasn't *only* talking about himself. He knew that he would be with God forever, but he was also talking about someone from his own family who would come a long time after him: Jesus. He remembered God's promise that one of his descendants would be king forever: 'Your house and your kingdom shall endure forever before me; your throne shall be established forever' (2 Samuel 7:16).

Luke – the writer of the book of Acts – says that David knew he was talking about the resurrection of Jesus because David was a prophet (as well as being a king), and God had told him that Jesus would be saved from death and would be king forever. Jesus did really die. But decay is what happens to a body when it has been in the ground a long time and Jesus was only in the ground for parts of three days until he was raised from the dead.[8]

Jesus wasn't abandoned by God to the grave; even though he died, he was raised from death. Unlike Lazarus, who had to die a second time after Jesus raised him to life, Jesus didn't die a second time. He was taken directly back to heaven by God the Father, forty days after he rose from the dead.

APPLICATION: If we know God then, like David, we can know that our Saviour Jesus is king forever, guiding and protecting us and one day giving us great joy from being with him in heaven.

It is good to know that when we trust God, we are not trusting someone who *used* to be king, or who *might* be king in the future, but we are trusting someone who *is* king now.

PRAYER: God, thank you that you kept your promise to King David when you sent Jesus, David's descendant, to be king forever. Thank you that Jesus can be my king too, and please help me to trust in you for everything that I need. Amen.

---

8. Jesus died on Friday and was raised on Sunday, so why does the writer say "three days and three nights"? Ancient Jews would refer to *any part* of a day as being 'a day and a night'. So to them, the Friday through Sunday - because it was part of three days - was referred to as "three days and three nights".

JESUS: PEOPLE WATCHED HIM DIE

MAY
22

PROPHET/DATES: King David, around 1000 BC.

PROPHECY MADE: 'Dogs surround me, a pack of villains encircles me; they pierce my hands and my feet. All my bones are on display; people stare and gloat over me. They divide my clothes among them and cast lots for my garment' (Psalm 22:16-18).

THEN AND THERE: King David was feeling alone, troubled and helpless. He didn't complain at God but cried out for his presence as he didn't feel that God was with him protecting him. David knew that it is only God who could bring him out of the terrible situation he was in.

David painted a picture of a completely hopeless and humiliating situation in which he was close to death. He was obviously very hungry because his 'bones are on display', meaning he has almost no fat or muscle left. He described himself as injured and surrounded by dogs – they would be there because they think there will soon be a dead body that they can have for food.

'cast lots for my garment' meant that people were gambling against each other to see who would get his clothes – clothes they thought he wouldn't need because he would soon be dead. We don't know whether that ever happened to David literally, but it is a picture of how bad his situation had become. One thousand years later however, those things would happen exactly as David wrote about them in his song, except they would happen to someone else.

PROPHECY FULFILLED: 'Those who passed by hurled insults at him, shaking their heads and saying, "So! You who are going to destroy the temple and build it in three days, come down from the cross and save yourself!"' (Mark 15:29-30).

'When the soldiers crucified Jesus, they took his clothes, dividing them into four shares, one for each of them, with the undergarment remaining. This garment was seamless, woven in one piece from top to bottom. "Let's not tear it," they said to one another. "Let's decide by lot who will get it." This happened that the scripture might be fulfilled which said, "They divided my clothes among them and cast lots for my garment"' (John 19:23-24).

SCARLET THREAD: When the Romans crucified people they deliberately did it in a very public place to act as a warning to other people not to commit any crimes that would risk such a horrible punishment. Jesus, and the two criminals with him, were crucified on top of a hill just outside the city of Jerusalem. Lots of people were interested to see this terrible thing and many of them liked to laugh, make fun of or shout insults at the people on the crosses. That's what happened to Jesus and the two men.

Having taken most of Jesus' clothes off him first, the soldiers who killed Jesus then played a gambling game to see who would get to keep those clothes. So what David gave as a picture of what was happening to himself, is exactly what happened to Jesus

He was humiliated, physically alone, greatly troubled, and seemingly helpless with lots of people around him who were happy to see that he was dying.

APPLICATION: It's easy to forget how much suffering Jesus went through so that his people could be saved from their sins. It was not just physical pain – these verses talk about being insulted and made fun of and made to look worthless. Have you thanked Jesus recently for being willing to do all that for you?

When people made fun of Jesus by challenging him to prove that he was Israel's true king, by coming down off the cross, it must have been extremely tempting for him. After all, he *was* God, so he *could* have come down off that cross if he wanted to and saved himself from incredible suffering. But it was his love for his Father God, and his love for his people that kept him there.

PRAYER: God, thank you that Jesus willingly went through all that suffering so that if we repent of our sins, we can be completely forgiven forever. Thank you that he didn't give up, didn't change his mind, and didn't decide that we weren't worth the sacrifice. Please help us never to take that for granted. Amen.

(12)

JESUS: THE SON OF DAVID

MAY
22

PROPHET/DATES: Nathan, around 1000 BC.

PROPHECY MADE: 'When your days are over and you rest with your ancestors, I will raise up your offspring to succeed you, your own flesh and blood, and I will establish his kingdom. He is the one who will build a house for my Name, and I will establish the throne of his kingdom forever. I will be his father, and he shall be my son. When he does wrong, I will punish him with a rod wielded by men, with floggings inflicted by human hands. But my love will never be taken away from him, as I took it away from Saul, whom I removed from before you. Your house and your kingdom shall endure for ever before me; your throne shall be established for ever' (2 Samuel 7:12-16).

THEN AND THERE: David was a war king, famous for his military victories, bravery and the people he killed, such as Goliath. When he had defeated Israel's enemies and there was no war going on, he told the prophet Nathan that he wanted to build a temple for God. The Israelites were still worshipping God using a tent ('Tabernacle') as they had done for 400 years since the Exodus from Egypt.

The prophet Nathan knew that God blessed everything David did, and that David's desire to build God a temple was a good one, so he advised David to go ahead. But God had other ideas. He gave Nathan a message to pass on to David, part of which

was to say, 'I have never complained about the tent before, and I've never commanded anyone to build me an expensive temple. I have blessed you in amazing ways, I will make you great and bless my people.' God said that David's son would be king after him in a land that was at peace, giving David peace of mind about the two things he was most concerned about.

That prophecy was fulfilled with David's son Solomon. He became king after David, ruled over a peaceful country, and built an expensive and impressive temple for God just as God commanded him. However, late in Solomon's life he disobeyed God in many ways including building places for the worship of false gods. God then raised up enemies to fight against Solomon – foreign enemies but also one of his own officials, called Jereboam. However, just as the prophecy said, the punishment wasn't total – Solomon still passed the kingship to his son Reheboam and God did not abandon Solomon.

PROPHECY FULFILLED: 'So [Jesus] became as much superior to the angels as the name he has inherited is superior to theirs. For to which of the angels did God ever say, "You are my Son; today I have become your Father"? Or again, "I will be his Father, and he will be my Son"?' (Hebrews 1:4-5).

'He will be great and will be called the Son of the Most High. The Lord God will give him the throne of his father David, and he will reign over Jacob's descendants forever; his kingdom will never end' (Luke 1:32-33).

SCARLET THREAD: Jesus was never an earthly king. When Jesus was on earth, Herod was the King of Israel and even tried to kill Jesus when Jesus was still a baby, thinking wrongly that when Jesus grew up he would try and get rid of Herod so that he could be king.

Jesus is a king though – not just a king of Israel but the king of everything, forever. The whole universe belongs to him even though he doesn't have a throne on earth. That's the way the prophecy given to David was fulfilled; someone from his family line – a Jew – would end up being king forever. Jesus is king now, and if we have asked him to forgive our sins then one day we will rule with him over the whole of God's creation.

But doesn't the prophecy also say that 'when he does wrong', God would punish him? Of course, Jesus never did anything wrong – he is the perfect Son of God, but God treated him as if he had done all the wrong of everybody who says sorry to God. God the Father put all those sins on Jesus – that was what was happening on the cross. God can forgive people, because the punishment for their sins has already been suffered by Jesus.

APPLICATION: Most stories about heroes are not kings but individual soldiers, because for hundreds of years the kings stayed well away from battle to avoid any chance of being killed. Not so with Jesus. He didn't *risk* being killed, he *knew* he'd be killed, just like the prophecy said he would be, and that's why we thank him so much. He has sacrificed more and done more for us than even the biggest war heroes.

We can thank God that even though Jesus is king, he was willing to take the punishment for all the sins of other people – all those people who have asked God to forgive their sin. Does that include you? Have you asked God to forgive your sin? If you have, it's thanks to God keeping this promise that your sins have been forgiven.

PRAYER: God, thank you that you kept your promise to King David. Not only did his family continue to rule Israel, but your son Jesus is now king over everything. Help me to treat him as my king, to be sorry for the bad thoughts, words and actions that I have and do. Thank you for forgiveness. Help me to obey Jesus' instructions. Amen.

JESUS: REJECTED WITHOUT REASON BY HIS ENEMIES

MAY 22

PROPHET/DATES: King David, around 1000 BC.

PROPHECY MADE: 'Those who hate me without reason outnumber the hairs of my head; many are my enemies without cause, those who seek to destroy me' (Psalm 69:4).

THEN AND THERE: When King David wrote this psalm he was having a bad time. I mean, *really* bad. Here's what he says in the first three verses of the psalm: 'Save me, O God, for the waters have come up to my neck. I sink in the miry depths, where there is no foothold. I have come into the deep waters; the floods engulf me. I am worn out calling for help; my throat is parched. My eyes fail, looking for my God.'

King David's enemies were so many and so strong that he felt sooner or later he was going to be defeated and killed. It felt so hopeless it made him think of drowning in quicksand, sinking down as the water rises up and God – seemingly – not listening to him.

What made it worse was that he felt there was no reason for them to hate him, and that he had done nothing to deserve it. It's hard to suffer – it's harder to suffer when we

feel it isn't fair, like being punished when we know we are innocent. But, although the psalm starts very unhappily, like many other psalms the message doesn't stay sad the whole way through. The reason David wrote the psalm was that God *did* rescue him, and David *didn't* end up being defeated. Those feelings of drowning went away. So much so that David was able to say, 'I will praise God's name in song and glorify him with thanksgiving'.

PROPHECY FULFILLED: '…they have seen, and yet they have hated both me and my Father. But this is to fulfil what is written in their Law: "They hated me without reason"' (John 15:24-25).

SCARLET THREAD: King David had been talking about himself, but through the Holy Spirit he was also making a prophecy about what would happen when the Messiah came much later. That was revealed to John while he was writing his book about Jesus and his message.

King David felt like he had done nothing to deserve people becoming his enemies. There was some truth in that because he was a man who tried to honour God and who defended his people. But David was a sinner so he wasn't totally correct.

For Jesus though, it was completely true that his enemies "hated [him] without reason". Jesus was perfect and did literally nothing wrong … not even a little bit, not even once. What's more, the only reason he had come to earth was to help people – by healing them of their sicknesses and providing them with food and teaching during his three years of public ministry, and especially by being the sacrifice for their sins so that they could be forgiven.

Jesus told his disciples that many people would hate them too – just like many hated him. He said that they must help each other a lot and stay obedient to God, especially during those tough times. Imagine that: Jesus – God himself – being willing to come to earth to save us from our sin, knowing that he would be hated by people for no reason.

And yet the story doesn't end with the religious leaders also hating Jesus … they killed him. This didn't take God by surprise though. Not only did God raise Jesus from the dead three days after he was killed, but it was Jesus' death and resurrection that means our sins can be forgiven and we can have a certain hope of life with God forever. It was Jesus being punished for our sins that means – if we are trusting in God – we don't face eternal punishment.

APPLICATION: Can you imagine hating someone who spent all their time trying to help you? Or has anyone ever said or done bad things to you and you don't understand why? Imagine how the psalmist felt when he was surrounded by people like that. Then remember that Jesus was murdered because people hated him for no reason. It's at times like that we need to turn to God for comfort because no matter how unfair people are, God is always there for us if we are trusting in him. And we don't have to just sit and think how sad it is that Jesus died. As we have learned, God raised him from the dead and Jesus' death means life for us.

PRAYER: Thank you, God, that Jesus was prepared to be hated by people for no reason, because he loved you and us enough to go through with it. Thank you that he didn't give up just because it was so unfair on him and he didn't deserve the hatred he received. Thank you that he obeyed you right to the end. Help me never to hate people, and to ask you for comfort if and when people hate me. Amen.

14

JESUS: REJECTED BY THE RELIGIOUS LEADERS

MAY
22

PROPHET/DATES: An anonymous psalmist, about 1,000 years before Jesus came to earth.

PROPHECY MADE: 'The stone the builders rejected has become the cornerstone; the LORD has done this, and it is marvellous in our eyes. The LORD has done it this very day; let us rejoice today and be glad' (Psalm 118:22-24).

THEN AND THERE: How do you show someone you are grateful for what they do for you? The author of these verses was writing a song to thank and praise God for his love, especially in rescuing the Jews from slavery in Egypt. After the rescue, God told them how important it was that they worshipped *only* him, obeyed him and looked after each other.

In this psalm, 'builders' refers to leaders, and the cornerstone was the most important stone in the foundations of a building. So the psalmist was saying that the leaders rejected the most important person: God. The leaders thought God was just one of many options. They liked the other options better, such as following false gods and pretending to follow the true God while disobeying him.

Amazingly, and despite all that, God in his great mercy had been kind to the Israelites, and saved them from their enemies many times. He showed himself to be the most important part of their lives. The psalm encourages God's people to be grateful for that.

 PROPHECY FULFILLED: 'Jesus said to them, "Have you never read in the Scriptures: 'The stone the builders rejected has become the cornerstone; the Lord has done this, and it is marvellous in our eyes'? ... When the chief priests and the Pharisees heard Jesus' parables, they knew he was talking about them' (Matthew 21:42 & 45).

 SCARLET THREAD: Many people loved Jesus, but not many of the leaders did. Some of them even hated him and wanted him dead. A lot of the Jews were waiting for someone awesome to come along and rescue them from the Roman invaders. So the less impressive that Jesus looked, (he was poor, and unpopular with the 'important' people) the less it looked to them like he was the kind of Messiah they were hoping for.

Just because people reject something or someone … doesn't mean they should. And just because the religious leaders rejected Jesus, it doesn't mean he wasn't God.

 APPLICATION: How do you feel when people, at school or in your group of friends, think one way and you want to think a different way? Maybe it's something small like a TV show you like that other people think is silly. Do you pretend you don't like it after all? Perhaps you just make sure not to talk about it.

It can be like that with King Jesus sometimes. We might know in our hearts and our minds from the Bible that Jesus is the Son of God who rose from the dead, but if lots of people around us think that's a silly idea, we start to doubt. Well, don't worry. Just because lots of people think that something isn't true, doesn't mean they're right. Equally, just because everyone thinks something *is* true, doesn't mean it is. Did you know, lots of people used to think the earth was flat? For thousands of years people just thought the sun went down and up, and didn't realise that we were going around it.

So if you know that Jesus is God and everyone else around you doesn't, that's OK. Jesus didn't say he would look cool, or that everyone would like him or agree with him. He said that many people would *not* believe in him, and may look down on you if *you* believe in him.

Many people think that Jesus was just an ordinary man in history who said some interesting things – such as being like a 'stone the builders rejected'. In reality, he is the 'cornerstone' – the most important part of life. If we don't build our lives around Jesus, starting with putting our trust in him, then the whole house of our life will not be right.

 PRAYER: Lord, please help me not to ignore Jesus because other people don't believe in him or because he didn't do anything that looks exciting, like fighting big battles or leading a country. Help me to know that he is the most important person ever, that he is your eternal Son, and that the best thing I can do is to trust him. Amen.

MAJOR AND MINOR PROPHETS

15

JESUS: HE DIED AND ROSE AGAIN THREE DAYS LATER

MAY 22

PROPHET/DATES: Jonah, around 750-725 BC.

PROPHECY MADE: 'Now the LORD provided a huge fish to swallow Jonah, and Jonah was in the belly of the fish three days and three nights … And the LORD commanded the fish, and it vomited Jonah onto dry land' (Jonah 1:17 & 2:10).

'Then some of the Pharisees and teachers of the law said to him, "Teacher, we want to see a sign from you." He answered, "A wicked and adulterous generation asks for a sign! But none will be given it except the sign of the prophet Jonah. For as Jonah was three days and three nights in the belly of a huge fish[9], so the Son of Man will be three days and three nights in the heart of the earth"' (Matthew 12:38-40).

---

9. There was a big storm on the boat that Jonah was in when he was running away from doing what God told him. Jonah told the people to throw him into the sea because the storm was his fault. He said God was punishing all of them with the storm because of Jonah. After they threw him in, God sent a big fish which swallowed Jonah, and three days later spat him out on dry land.

THEN AND THERE: Jonah wasn't a hero. When we first read about him God had said, 'Tell the people in the city of Nineveh that they are going to be punished for their sins'. Jonah responded by setting sail in the opposite direction: he hated the people of Nineveh because they were evil and he thought if he went and told them about God, that God would end up taking pity on them and forgiving them and Jonah didn't want that.

Later, after the famous incident with the big fish, the book about Jonah ends with the prophet unhappy and angry again. Jonah complains that the shady plant God provided for him has shrivelled up. Clearly, the point of the story is *not* to be like Jonah!

Jonah did not speak words of a prophecy that were directly about Jesus, but the most famous incident in his life was an early picture of what would happen to Jesus. It wasn't a coincidence – Jesus himself said that what happened to Jonah pointed to what was going to happen to him.

PROPHECY FULFILLED: 'For what I received I passed on to you as of first importance: that Christ died for our sins according to the Scriptures, that he was buried, that he was raised on the third day according to the Scriptures, and that he appeared to Cephas [Peter], and then to the Twelve [disciples]. After that, he appeared to more than five hundred of the brothers and sisters at the same time …' (1 Corinthians 15:3-6).

SCARLET THREAD: Jesus rose again on the third day. Friday, when he was crucified, was the first day. Saturday was the second day and Sunday the third. Paul points that out not because it was a fun fact for somebody, but because it all happened just as God said it would ('according to the Scriptures'). Paul confirmed what Jesus had said, that the events of Jonah's life were a picture-prophecy of what would happen to Jesus. Jesus rising on the third day was part of the fulfilment of that prophecy and another piece of evidence that everything God says will happen, happens.

The first part of Paul's missionary life was to his fellow Jews. Most of them were still waiting for the Messiah to come for the *first* time, because they had not accepted Jesus. Paul therefore spent a lot of time with them comparing what happened to Jesus with all the prophecies about the Messiah in the Old Testament. He 'baffled the Jews … by proving that Jesus is the Messiah' (Acts 9:22).

The Jews were also the main target audience for Matthew's gospel. That's why he included the long genealogy at the start of his gospel – to show them how Jesus didn't come randomly out of nowhere. Jesus was from the line of families that the Messiah was prophesied to come from.

It all made sense, it all fitted together. Jesus was who he said he was, and he was who the prophecies said he would be.

APPLICATION: When lawyers represent a client in court, they don't say to the judge, 'Look your honour, I've found one piece of evidence. Is that enough for you?'. They try to find witnesses and lots of pieces of evidence to prove they are right.

When God told people about the coming of the Messiah he didn't just leave one piece of evidence. Apart from the thousands of witnesses of Jesus' miracles, and the hundreds of witnesses of Jesus' rising from the dead, we have hundreds of prophecies that all come true in Jesus.

God could have just said 'I'll give you *one* piece of evidence and that should be enough.' After all, it's God, right? We should believe him … right? But instead of that, God gave us so much more, including the life of Jonah that God used as a symbol – even giving us the timing of Jesus' resurrection.

When Jonah was thrown into the sea, that was the symbol of Jesus' death.

When Jonah was swallowed by the whale/big fish, that was the symbol of Jesus' burial.

When Jonah was in the fish until the third day, that was the symbol of Jesus being buried from Friday until Sunday.

When Jonah was spat out onto land by the big fish, that was the symbol of Jesus coming out of the tomb again … alive!

There is so much proof of who Jesus was and is; it would be enough for any judge. Is it enough for you to believe that he is who he says he is?

PRAYER: Thank you, God, that you have provided so many different pieces of evidence that Jesus is your Son, and that he was sent by you. Thank you for the story of Jonah which points to Jesus. And thank you most of all that you *did* raise him to life again, giving Jesus and us the victory over death. Amen.

The stone the builders rejected ...

... the sign of the prophet Jonah.

 ... your throne will be established forever.

They divide my clothes among them ...

... you will not abandon me to the realm of the dead.

16

JESUS: BORN OF A VIRGIN

PROPHET/DATES: Isaiah around 740-680 BC.

PROPHECY MADE: 'Therefore the Lord himself will give you a sign. Behold, the virgin shall conceive and bear a son, and shall call his name Immanuel. He shall eat curds and honey when he knows how to refuse the evil and choose the good' (Isaiah 7:14-16 ESV).

THEN AND THERE: The northern kingdom of Israel (all the tribes except Judah) had been attacked and defeated by the Assyrians before this prophecy. A few years later, Judah was attacked by Aramites, helped by Israelites!

It was no surprise that 'the hearts of Ahaz and his people were shaken, as the trees of the forest are shaken by the wind' (Isaiah 7:2). They were terrified and felt like they were betrayed and had no hope. After all, although the country had split 300 years earlier, the idea of Israelites attacking Judah was unthinkable.

God sent Isaiah and his son to encourage King Ahaz of Judah, telling him that although his enemies were plotting his defeat: 'It will not take place, it will not happen' (Isaiah 7:7). Isaiah, however, warned Ahaz how important it was to stay faithful to God: 'If you do not stand firm in your faith, you will not stand at all' (Isaiah 7:9).

To encourage King Ahaz to stand firm and believe in God's promise of deliverance, God said that the lady about to become Isaiah's second wife would have a son – to be known as 'Immanuel'. Before the son was old enough to talk, the enemies of Judah would be wiped out by another enemy, so that Judah would be safe.

Imagine how excited the people would have been when they saw Isaiah's wife having a baby, to think that soon they would be free from their enemies!

PROPHECY FULFILLED: '... an angel of the Lord appeared to him in a dream and said, "Joseph son of David, do not be afraid to take Mary home as your wife, because what is conceived in her is from the Holy Spirit. She will give birth to a son, and you are to give him the name Jesus, because he will save his people from their sins".

All this took place to fulfil what the Lord had said through the prophet: "The virgin will conceive and give birth to a son, and they will call him Immanuel," (which means "God with us")' (Matthew 1:20-23).

SCARLET THREAD: Seven hundred years after Isaiah's son was born, there was a young lady called Mary about to become the wife of a man named Joseph. Before they got married, she became pregnant and gave birth to a son, called Jesus. It was scary for Joseph – he was worried at first that Mary had been unfaithful to him. However, an angel of God told him no, Mary was pregnant without going to bed with a man, through the power of God. Because of that miracle, no-one could argue that the baby Jesus was an ordinary man who people pretended was important. They could see that Jesus was God himself come down to earth.

When Mary and Joseph had the baby, they were told by an angel to call him Jesus, 'because he will save his people from their sins' (Matthew 1:21). That makes sense, because the name Jesus means, 'God is the one who saves'. 'Immanuel', another name that Jesus was known by, means 'God with us'.

APPLICATION: The first time I was in a nativity play I was about four years old. I was playing the part of the star that the wise men followed, so it was not a hard part, but I was very nervous! I don't think I paid much attention to the Bible story that day, which is a pity because the miracle of Jesus being born to a virgin was the most wonderful thing that had ever happened.

Why do you think Jesus came to earth? What did he come here to do?

PRAYER: Thank you, God, that Jesus was born as a special miracle baby, showing that he really is God with us. Thank you that the boy was and is your son Jesus, who came down to live a perfect life on earth before dying to save his people from their sins. Amen.

* The picture here is a visual representation of the prophecy as it was understood by the people of the time. In this picture the woman and boy represent Isaiah's wife and son. The shadow represents what was going to happen, in that Judah's enemies would be wiped out and Judah would be safe.

17

JESUS: MEEK AND HUMBLE

MAY
22

PROPHET/DATES: Isaiah around 740-680 BC.

PROPHECY MADE: 'Here is my servant, whom I uphold, my chosen one in whom I delight; I will put my Spirit on him and he will bring justice to the nations. He will not shout or cry out, or raise his voice in the streets. A bruised reed he will not break, and a smouldering wick he will not snuff out. In faithfulness he will bring forth justice; he will not falter or be discouraged till he establishes justice on earth. In his teaching the islands will put their hope' (Isaiah 42:1-4).

THEN AND THERE: This is what a godly leader looks like, this is what he does, and God delights in him. In the previous chapter God was talking about King Darius, who would defeat the wicked Babylonian King Belshazzar and start the chain of events

ending in the Israelites going back to their homes after seventy years in exile. The verses are also about what God was planning to do in and through godly leaders, and God's desire for the Israelites to lead the world in spreading the message about God, showing justice and godliness to the world.[10]

But it also points to someone who is above all that, because the whole world is putting its hope in his law, and you can only do that when you are looking at God's perfect law.

PROPHECY FULFILLED: '... A large crowd followed him, and he healed all who were ill. He warned them not to tell others about him. This was to fulfil what was spoken through the prophet Isaiah: "Here is my servant whom I have chosen, the one I love, in whom I delight; I will put my Spirit on him, and he will proclaim justice to the nations. He will not quarrel or cry out; no one will hear his voice in the streets. A bruised reed he will not break, and a smouldering wick he will not snuff out, till he has brought justice through to victory. In his name the nations will put their hope"' (Matthew 12:15-21).

SCARLET THREAD: When you blow out a candle, the top of the wick is still very hot, with smoke coming off, even though the flame has gone. To stop the smoke, you can pinch the wick with your fingers – that's what it means to snuff out a smouldering wick. In this prophecy picture, a smouldering wick is a person, and the flame is their relationship with God. Even if a person is nearly gone away completely from God, and maybe they're not doing anything useful with their life, God doesn't say to them he's not interested any more. He wants everyone to come to him to have their sins forgiven and enjoy life with him forever.

Jesus wasn't interested in becoming an earthly leader. He wasn't aggressive; he didn't have shouting matches with the Pharisees even though many of them were awful people with no love for God or for people. Jesus didn't come to be popular – he came in love to bring truth, healing and justice. In him, people all over the world put their hope.

APPLICATION: God wants you to know him, and he's not measuring how good you are already, or how much you love him already. He brought justice by providing hope for every person, not just the rich and powerful. He also brought justice by being the sacrifice – the punishment – for the sins of all those who put their trust in him.

Have you put your hope in Jesus?

PRAYER: God, thank you that Jesus brought justice and mercy through the way that he lived and through his sacrifice. Thank you that he did that while being meek and humble: obeying you and loving people always with kindness even when it was hard, and never pushing away someone who wanted to know him. Thank you that he is the same way now. Amen.

---

10. Isaiah 66:19-21

JESUS: HE CAST OUT DEMONS AND HEALED PEOPLE

MAY
22

PROPHET/DATES: Isaiah, around 700 BC.

PROPHECY MADE: 'Strengthen the feeble hands, steady the knees that give way; say to those with fearful hearts, "Be strong, do not fear; your God will come, he will come with vengeance; with divine retribution he will come to save you." Then will the eyes of the blind be opened and the ears of the deaf unstopped. Then will the lame leap like a deer, and the mute tongue shout for joy. Water will gush forth in the wilderness and streams in the desert' (Isaiah 35:3-6).

THEN AND THERE: Isaiah's prophecy is scary in some places. Most of what he said to God's people was hard for them to hear. This is because of all the warnings about punishment if they kept disobeying God. He was giving them more opportunity to be sorry, and turn back to him.

Amazingly, even though God knew they would keep disobeying him, he still promised that one day he would bring them back from their punishment. He even promised that their enemies would be defeated.

When your parents love you, there are times when they need to punish you. They don't enjoy that, and they may give you many opportunities to do the right thing so that the punishment doesn't need to happen. But when punishment does happen, it is there to remind you that you need to come back to God, and that sin is a very serious thing that gets in between you and God.

The blessings God promised the Israelites were not ordinary: he said that amazing things would happen, like blind people being able to see, and people who can't even walk being able to jump up like a springing deer!

PROPHECY FULFILLED: '[Jesus] went to Nazareth, where he had been brought up, and on the Sabbath day he went into the synagogue, as was his custom. He stood up to read, and the scroll of the prophet Isaiah was handed to him. Unrolling it, he found the place where it is written: "The Spirit of the Lord is on me, because he has anointed me to proclaim good news to the poor. He has sent me to proclaim freedom for the prisoners and recovery of sight for the blind, to set the oppressed free, to proclaim the year of the Lord's favour." Then he rolled up the scroll, gave it back to the attendant and sat down. The eyes of everyone in the synagogue were fastened on him. He began by saying to them, "Today this scripture is fulfilled in your hearing"' (Luke 4:16-21).

'When John, who was in prison, heard about the deeds of the Messiah, he sent his disciples to ask him, "Are you the one who is to come, or should we expect someone else?" Jesus replied, "Go back and report to John what you hear and see: the blind receive sight, the lame walk, those who have leprosy are cleansed, the deaf hear, the dead are raised, and the good news is proclaimed to the poor"' (Matthew 11:2-5).

SCARLET THREAD: It's not hard to see how Isaiah's prophecy is about Jesus, because Jesus stood up and said that it was. It doesn't get any clearer than that!

Jesus performed many miracles during his three years of ministry. He made blind people to see; he made people who couldn't walk, able to dance immediately. He cured sick people of their disease, and he made deaf people to hear. He even raised dead people to life – everything that Isaiah said would happen, and more. He also preached 'good news … to the poor' (Luke 4:18).

The 'good news' was not that Jesus was about to give them some money – that would only help them a little bit while they were still on earth. Jesus' good news was way better than that. It was the news that because of God's love for them, their sins could be forgiven *forever*. That they could be with God *forever*. That their broken relationship with God could be fixed *forever*. That's the best news that anyone could ever have, and Jesus didn't come to give that news mainly to rich people who might give him money for telling them nice things. Instead, Jesus went first and mainly to the poor people, and told them all about it.

APPLICATION: Jesus did miracles so that people would know who he was. He could have done anything he wanted: like making a mountain go up in the air, or making stars move. Instead, he did miracles that really helped people, because he cares for and loves people. Do you know that he cares about you?

Jesus' answer to John's question, 'Are you the Messiah?' was a challenge for John to check things out for himself. Jesus wanted him to see the evidence of what Jesus was doing compared to what was prophesied. Jesus didn't come from nowhere, he came just as God promised he would, and that's what he was telling John and everyone else. God was saving his people, just like he said. You too can see how God has done everything he said he would, and you can therefore know that God can be trusted.

PRAYER: God, thank you that you love your people so much, and for all Jesus' kindness in helping people, proving who he is. Help me to listen to the good news that Jesus brought. Amen.

(19)

JESUS: BORN IN BETHLEHEM

MAY 22

PROPHET/DATES: Micah, about 700-750 years before Jesus.

PROPHECY MADE: 'But you, Bethlehem Ephrathah, though you are small among the clans of Judah, out of you will come for me one who will be ruler over Israel, whose origins are from of old, from ancient times' (Micah 5:2).

THEN AND THERE: Bethlehem was a small town near Jerusalem, famous because King David was from there. At the time of the prophecy God's people were not obeying him – they were worshipping false gods and failing to take care of people in need. Micah was one of a number of prophets sent by God to warn his people about that. God promised that there would be a terrible punishment, but that he would bring them out

of that punishment. Soldiers would "strike Israel's ruler on the cheek with a rod," God said, but then gave this promise in Micah 5:2.

God was reassuring his people that although great punishment was coming because of their disobedience, God would bring a ruler over God's people, from Israel. That ruler would unite God's people, look after them, and bring peace and protection from their enemies.

PROPHECY FULFILLED: 'So Joseph also went up from the town of Nazareth in Galilee to Judea, to Bethlehem the town of David, because he belonged to the house and line of David. He went there to register with Mary, who was pledged to be married to him and was expecting a child. While they were there, the time came for the baby to be born, and she gave birth to her firstborn, a son' (Luke 2:4-7).

It would have looked more impressive if Jesus was born in Jerusalem, the capital city. However, God always does things in the wisest way, and that often means he picks people and places that are less impressive, less popular, or less good-looking than maybe we would pick, and he uses them to fulfil his great plans. For example, God said right from the start that he didn't pick Israel because they were a great nation, but he simply decided to love them and to keep his promises to them[11].

SCARLET THREAD: This prophecy almost didn't get fulfilled! Well, that's not really true because it was never in doubt that God would keep all of his promises, but it didn't look like it was going to happen until Jesus was already growing as a baby inside his mother. It was prophesied that Jesus would be born in Bethlehem, but Mary and her soon-to-be husband, Joseph, lived in Nazareth. However, the Romans decided to count everyone in Israel and told them to go back to where their families were originally from and be counted. Joseph's family had its roots in Bethlehem for at least 1,200 years since Boaz married Ruth and they had a son called Obed, who had a son called Jesse, whose son became King David. Because of that, Joseph and Mary had to walk all the way to Bethlehem – a journey of about 100 miles.

And when Jesus grew up, just like the prophecy said he became the ruler of his people; not the country of Israel but the 'Israel' that means all Christians – all people from all over the world who call God their Father and their Saviour and their Lord. They are Jesus' people and he rules over them.

APPLICATION: Do you think that you are not important enough for God, the creator of the whole universe, to be interested in you? Well … God *is* interested in you!

He showed repeatedly in the Bible that he is interested in *all* people, no matter how unimportant or young they are; Jesus even had to correct his disciples when they were trying to stop people taking their little children for Jesus to bless them (Matthew 19:13). Sometimes other people in your life might make you feel that you are not important to them, but you never need to feel like that with God.

PRAYER: Thank you, God, that you kept your promise about Jesus being born in Bethlehem and becoming the ruler of his people. Thank you that he is our ruler too if we put our trust in him. Amen.

---

11. Deuteronomy 7:7-8

(20)

JESUS AND HIS FAMILY ESCAPED TO EGYPT

PROPHET/DATES: Hosea, 740 years before Jesus.

PROPHECY MADE: 'When Israel was a child, I loved him, and out of Egypt I called my son' (Hosea 11:1).

THEN AND THERE: For the 400 years the Israelites were in Egypt, they grew into a nation of over one million people, who God called his 'child' or 'son'.[12] One thousand, two hundred years before this prophecy was the 'Exodus', when God rescued his people from their slave-owners in Egypt, leading them out of the country and eventually into the Promised Land.

The verses after this, in the prophecy, talk about how God's people had ignored him and all he had done for them, how they would be punished for their sin but God would not destroy them completely because he loved them too much to do that.

12. Exodus 4:22; John 1:12-13

PROPHECY FULFILLED: 'So he got up, took the child and his mother during the night and left for Egypt, where he stayed until the death of Herod. And so was fulfilled what the Lord had said through the prophet: "Out of Egypt I called my son."

When Herod realised that he had been outwitted by the Magi, he was furious, and he gave orders to kill all the boys in Bethlehem and its vicinity who were two years old and under, in accordance with the time he had learned from the Magi.

After Herod died, an angel of the Lord appeared in a dream to Joseph in Egypt and said, "Get up, take the child and his mother and go to the land of Israel, for those who were trying to take the child's life are dead."

So he got up, took the child and his mother and went to the land of Israel'
(Matthew 2:14-16, 19-21).

SCARLET THREAD: Hosea didn't know that Jesus and his parents would run away to Egypt to escape being killed by their enemies in Israel. He probably thought it was more likely to happen the other way around – that someone would run away to Israel to escape their enemies in Egypt!

But King Herod (who was afraid that people would want to make Jesus the King of Israel instead of him) ordered that all the boys in Bethlehem of two years old or under be killed. He didn't know exactly when Jesus was born but he knew it had been less than two years and he wanted to make sure that Jesus was killed.

Eventually, while Jesus was still a young boy, King Herod died and the next King (also called Herod), wasn't bothered about killing Jesus, so Jesus' parents Mary and Joseph came back to their country of Israel.

God the Father was protecting his Son: first an angel appeared to Joseph in a dream to tell them to run away, and then the same thing happened to tell Joseph they could go back home. It doesn't matter how determined wicked people are to stop God and his plans to save his people, because God's loving plans cannot be stopped.

APPLICATION: Satan always wants to destroy God's plans, and he was most desperate to do that while Jesus was on earth. Herod's attempt to kill Jesus would have been defeat for God, but God wouldn't allow it. When Satan finally managed to have Jesus killed it was too late, because Jesus' death was part of God's plan to save his people from their sins.

Satan doesn't want you to know God. The biggest danger isn't a modern day King Herod trying to kill you, but it's that we can be kept away from God by our own brain. We can forget about God or try to get close to God by what we think is best, rather than what God has said in the Bible.

What stops you wanting to pray and read your Bible so that you can get to know God better?

PRAYER: Father God, thank you for protecting your Son Jesus and his parents so that they could escape to Egypt, and then bringing them back to Israel so that Jesus could be the Saviour of his people. Please help me to trust you always and not to be tempted to ignore you or do things on my own without your strength and guidance. Amen.

21

JESUS: THE SON OF MAN

MAY 22

PROPHET/DATES: Daniel, in about 539 BC.

PROPHECY MADE: 'In my vision at night I looked, and there before me was one like a son of man, coming with the clouds of heaven. He approached the Ancient of Days and was led into his presence. He was given authority, glory and sovereign power; all nations and peoples of every language worshipped him. His dominion is an everlasting dominion that will not pass away, and his kingdom is one that will never be destroyed' (Daniel 7:13-14).

THEN AND THERE: Daniel and the other people of Judah were victims of the Babylonian invasion, taken captive in 597 BC and forced to go and live in the country of their enemies. Daniel prayed openly to God in Babylon, even though there was a law saying he was not allowed to do that. As punishment he was thrown into a den of lions to be eaten, but even though the lions were extremely hungry they didn't even touch him, because God was protecting him.

Sixty years after going to Babylon, and with a successful and long career behind him working for the rulers of Babylon, Daniel was given visions by God. It was like having dreams while you're still awake; God was describing pictures and events to Daniel.

The people of Israel were there because they disobeyed God badly for hundreds of years: worshipping idols, neglecting the needy, taking money from the poor, refusing

to look after the helpless. But in the middle of their punishment, when they might have worried that God couldn't help them because he wasn't strong enough, or had forgotten them, God gave Daniel this vision.

Through this vision God told his people that he was still God. He would be worshipped by people from all over the world and would give all his authority to someone who was a man … but not just a man. That person would rule forever and nobody and nothing would be able to defeat him or take him off into captivity (unlike the Babylonians who had defeated the Assyrians and the Israelites but were then defeated by the Persians). The Israelites didn't need to feel that all was lost, as if their God had been defeated – he hadn't, and the 'Son of Man' who God would send, would rule forever.

Not long after the prophecy, the Jews started to return to Israel and they knew this prophecy was about much more than that. The righteous and almighty rule of the 'Son of Man' was something the Jews were looking forward to. In the 600 years between the prophecy and when Jesus came to earth, nobody had yet fitted that description. Still they looked forward to the day of fulfilment.

PROPHECY FULFILLED: Jesus replied, 'Foxes have dens and birds have nests, but the Son of Man has nowhere to lay his head' (Matthew 8:20).

'… and among the lampstands was someone like a son of man … [he said] … "… Do not be afraid. I am the First and the Last. I am the Living One; I was dead, and now look, I am alive for ever and ever! And I hold the keys of death and Hades"' (Revelation 1:13, 17-18).

'I looked, and there before me was a white cloud, and seated on the cloud was one like a son of man with a crown of gold on his head …' (Revelation 14:14).

SCARLET THREAD: Jesus spent a lot of time proving to people that he was God, and he also told them many times. Claiming to be the 'Son of Man' was Jesus claiming to be God, because everyone knew that the Son of Man was God himself. After all, no one but God can rule forever with the authority given him by God the Father, and no one but God should be worshipped by people from all over the world.

APPLICATION: When I put my money into the bank to be looked after, I like to be sure that it's safe. That's one of the reasons we use banks – so that we don't have to keep paper money in our homes or carry it around and risk it getting lost or stolen.

When we decide what our life is going to be about, we need to be absolutely sure where we are putting our time, energy, thoughts, actions, emotions and efforts. If you decide that you want your life to be all about pleasing God – which is what you were designed to do – isn't it good to know that God can't be beaten and that he'll never go away? Trusting God is even more safe than keeping your money in the bank!

These verses remind us that the eternal God the Father spoke about his Son Jesus who would rule forever. Six hundred years after Daniel received his prophetic vision, Jesus came to earth to pay the price of our sins, he now rules in heaven, and one day he will come again to rule over everything.

PRAYER: Thank you, God, for your Son Jesus, the 'Son of Man', that you are giving him all the authority, all the power, all the glory. Thank you that he will rule forever and that we can be part of that if we repent of our sins and trust in you. Amen.

22

KING HEROD KILLED THE CHILDREN IN BETHLEHEM

MAY 22

PROPHET/DATES: Jeremiah, 550 BC.

PROPHECY MADE: 'This is what the LORD says: "A voice is heard in Ramah, mourning and great weeping, Rachel weeping for her children and refusing to be comforted, because they are no more"' (Jeremiah 31:15).

THEN AND THERE: Jeremiah was writing while the tribe of Judah – God's people – were being defeated by the Babylonian army. Many people were killed, and many others were taken away to Babylon as slaves.

Ramah was one of the places people passed through on the way to Babylon. Rachel was a wife of Jacob, and the twelve tribes of Israel all came from his sons and grandsons. Rachel is used here as a symbol of all God's people in the Old Testament – the Israelites.

These verses look like they are prophesying terrible things for God's people, but they were simply describing what was already going on at the time. The people he was sending a message to were incredibly sad and couldn't understand how they would ever be happy again because of all the death and destruction around them.

God sent Jeremiah a message to encourage them – before these verses it says, 'I will turn their mourning into gladness; I will give them comfort and joy instead of sorrow'. And two verses later: '... there is hope for your descendants ... Your children will return to their own land'.

God had heard the repentance of his people and he promised they would go back to their own country, a promise so good and so seemingly unlikely that they couldn't imagine it would happen.

PROPHECY FULFILLED: 'When Herod realised that he had been outwitted by the Magi, he was furious, and he gave orders to kill all the boys in Bethlehem and its vicinity who were two years old and under, in accordance with the time he had learned from the Magi. Then what was said through the prophet Jeremiah was fulfilled: "A voice is heard in Ramah, weeping and great mourning, Rachel weeping for her children and refusing to be comforted, because they are no more"' (Matthew 2:16-18).

SCARLET THREAD: Herod told the Wise Men ('Magi') to let him know where baby Jesus was, once they had found him. He told them it was so that he too could go celebrate the birth. However, he really wanted to kill Jesus because the Magi had mentioned Jesus was the 'king of the Jews'. Herod (who was king of the country at that time) thought that people were going to try and make Jesus king of the country instead of him – he didn't understand that Jesus wasn't going to do that. Jesus is in charge of *everything* because he is God, but Jesus didn't want to be leader of a country.

Because Herod thought Jesus was a threat he wanted to kill him, and when the Magi didn't tell him where to find Jesus he decided to kill all the young boys in the area who were born around the same time as Jesus – just to make sure that he killed Jesus.

God told the Magi in a dream to avoid Jerusalem (the city where Herod lived) on their way back to their own country. God also warned Jesus' parents that they needed to escape to Egypt.

This part of the prophecy was the sad part. It was good news for the people in Jeremiah's day, but terrible news for the people in Jesus' day.

APPLICATION: Do you remember what it is like to feel very sad? Maybe you even feel that way now. But sadness does not last forever when we have God, because if we have him, then we always have a reason for great joy and happiness.

Thank God that even though an awful thing was done by Herod, that Jesus escaped to Egypt with his parents Mary and Joseph, so that he was not killed.

Thank God that nothing can stop his plans from happening, and nothing can stop what he prophesied from coming true. Not even a murderous king like Herod.

PRAYER: God, please help us to trust you even when people are suffering or bad things are happening. And thank you that Jesus was kept safe even though the most powerful man in the whole country was trying to kill him. Amen.

23

JESUS: HIS DISCIPLES WERE SCATTERED

MAY 22

PROPHET/DATES: Zechariah, around 520-500 BC.

PROPHECY MADE: 'Awake, O sword, against my shepherd, against the man who stands next to me,' declares the LORD of hosts. 'Strike the shepherd, and the sheep will be scattered; I will turn my hand against the little ones' (Zechariah 13:7, ESV).

THEN AND THERE: In the previous verses Zechariah was telling the people that God would get rid of false prophets from the country (there were lots of them pretending to have a message from God but they were just making it up). He would also rid the land of idols and clean the people from their sin.

Those all sound like good things that God was going to do, although it probably wouldn't be fun while God was doing it, because many people were going to be punished. God then talked about his shepherd – the one who stands next to him or is close to him as a ruler. You might expect God to say nice things at this point, but instead he says that his shepherd must be attacked, and all the shepherd's sheep will run away.

There was no obvious meaning for the people who heard this right away. They knew that a prophecy was being made about the future. It seemed to involve terrible things happening to a man of God and those under his authority not having the courage to stick around when their leader was suffering.

It would have been scary for them and have reminded them that they needed to trust God because he always knows best.

PROPHECY FULFILLED: 'In that hour Jesus said to the crowd, "Am I leading a rebellion, that you have come out with swords and clubs to capture me? Every day I sat in the temple courts teaching, and you did not arrest me. But this has all taken place that the writings of the prophets might be fulfilled." Then all the disciples deserted him and fled' (Matthew 26:55-56).

SCARLET THREAD: After Judas Iscariot betrayed Jesus he led the religious leaders to Jesus in the Garden of Gethsemane. They brought a crowd of people with weapons in case Jesus or his disciples fought back. Peter started to do just that, cutting off the ear of the high priest's servant with his sword.

Jesus showed that the armed crowd were cowards and did not understand him at all, when he asked why they came at him with weapons as he had never threatened to hurt anybody. He even healed the High Priest's servant of his injury and so proved his point. Everything that was happening was to fulfil prophecies that had been made many years before.

What happened next was that the disciples – without meaning to – fulfilled another prophecy: they all ran away. They had been Jesus' closest friends for three years, had followed him around everywhere he went, through popular and unpopular times and without ever having much money. But now when their best friend, who they knew was sent by God, seemed to need them the most, they ran away.

APPLICATION: Following Jesus won't always be easy, and sometimes it will be very hard. You may never be as scared as the disciples were with all those people with weapons around them, but if you want to follow Jesus you will need God's strength and courage to help you.

It is easy to be discouraged if life seems to be getting difficult, or when bad things happen. That's when it is most important to remember that God never changes, never forgets his people, never stops loving them and never stops taking care of them. If the disciples had remembered that, they would not have felt the need to run away.

PRAYER: God, thank you that even though Jesus might have been scared too, he didn't run away like the disciples. Thank you that even though the idea of his suffering caused him great stress, he still went through with it because of his great love for you and for us. Please help me to love Jesus because of his great love. Amen.

24

JESUS: THE KING

MAY
22

PROPHET/DATES: Zechariah, around 520-500 BC.

PROPHECY MADE: 'Rejoice greatly, Daughter Zion! Shout, Daughter Jerusalem! See, your king comes to you, righteous and victorious, lowly and riding on a donkey, on a colt, the foal of a donkey' (Zechariah 9:9).

THEN AND THERE: In ancient times, after a king had been victorious in war he would return to his capital city in a victory parade with crowds greeting him. He would ride on a horse, with his soldiers and prisoners walking behind him. But the king in this prophecy, although victorious, showed that he was more humble by riding not on a beautiful big horse but on a young donkey which was much smaller and not as nice to look at.

Daughter Zion means Jerusalem, the capital of Israel, which was also a symbol of all of God's people.

Zechariah was prophesying after the Jews had returned from their exile. They were back in their own country but had again started worshipping false gods and ignoring the poor and needy people. Part of the prophecy was calling them to repent again and come back to God, and the other part was about the Messiah, who would one day come to save his people.

This encouraged the people, telling them that the Messiah would be a very godly king who would bring them a famous victory, but he wouldn't be obsessed with looking impressive – hence the donkey.

PROPHECY FULFILLED: 'This took place to fulfil what was spoken through the prophet: "Say to Daughter Zion, See, your king comes to you, gentle and riding on a donkey, and on a colt, the foal of a donkey"' (Matthew 21:4-5).

SCARLET THREAD: What is the 'This' that 'took place'? It was the arrangements Jesus gave for when he would be entering Jerusalem on Palm Sunday as the king who would have victory for all his people – just one week before he was murdered. Jesus' humility and gentleness showed that although he was a victorious king he was not a violent man. Fulfilling the prophecy was a glorious moment for all the Jews, and ultimately for all Jesus' people – Jews and Gentiles alike.

Sadly most of the people of Jerusalem didn't understand that the way Jesus was entering Jerusalem was fulfilling the prophecy from the psalms of Israel's conquering king. When people were asking who Jesus was, 'The crowds answered, "This is Jesus, the prophet from Nazareth in Galilee."'[13] So they were pleased to see him because they knew he was a godly man, but they didn't realise he was God himself.

APPLICATION: Who do you think that Jesus is? Are you like most of the Jews who thought Jesus was a good guy from God – probably a prophet, a good teacher with some interesting things to say? Or do you believe that he is a king, sent by God who won the victory so that his people can be saved?

PRAYER: Thank you, God, that Jesus is the king of his people; victorious over sin but also gentle and humble. Please help me to treat him as my king, as I should. Amen.

---

13. Matthew 21:11

25

THE PRICE OF BETRAYAL

MAY 22

PROPHET/DATES: Zechariah (about 500 BC) and Jeremiah (about 600-550 BC).

PROPHECY MADE: Jeremiah made several statements about Jesus' betrayal which Matthew refers to in his gospel (e.g. Matthew 9:1-13), but the most direct reference is in Zechariah: 'I told them, "If you think it best, give me my pay; but if not, keep it." So they paid me thirty pieces of silver. And the LORD said to me, "Throw it to the potter" – the handsome price at which they valued me! So I took the thirty pieces of silver and threw them to the potter at the house of the LORD' (Zechariah 11:12-13).

THEN AND THERE: Zechariah was one of the last prophets of Old Testament times. He prophesied in Judah after the people had returned from exile in Babylon, telling the people they needed to focus on their relationship with God. They had become quite happy disobeying God and no longer cared about worshipping him or being kind to poor people and others in need. Terrible things happened to God's people. These verses tell us about how God sent judgment on their leaders who didn't care about them. They had only recently come back from exile but their disobedience continued: further judgment was waiting for them if they didn't repent.

PROPHECY FULFILLED: 'Then one of the Twelve – the one called Judas Iscariot – went to the chief priests and asked, "What are you willing to give me if I deliver him over to you?" So they counted out for him thirty pieces of silver' (Matthew 26:14-15).

'When Judas, who had betrayed him, saw that Jesus was condemned, he was seized with remorse and returned the thirty pieces of silver to the chief priests and the elders. "I have sinned," he said, "for I have betrayed innocent blood." "What is that to us?" they replied. "That's your responsibility." So Judas threw the money into the temple and left. Then he went away and hanged himself.

The chief priests picked up the coins and said, "It is against the law to put this into the treasury, since it is blood money." So they decided to use the money to buy the potter's field as a burial place for foreigners. That is why it has been called the Field of Blood to this day. Then what was spoken by Jeremiah the prophet was fulfilled: "They took the thirty pieces of silver, the price set on him by the people of Israel, and they used them to buy the potter's field, as the Lord commanded me"' (Matthew 27:3-10).

SCARLET THREAD: These Old Testament prophecies about the betrayal of Jesus were fulfilled in several different ways:

Thirty pieces of silver: this was the price that the prophet had been promised as payment – before he broke the contract and said, 'Pay me or not.' Thirty pieces of silver was the standard price for a slave, and it was the price that the religious leaders paid Judas Iscariot when he agreed to betray Jesus.

threw [the coins] to the potter: when Judas – who regretted betraying Jesus – threw the money back at the religious leaders they didn't want to keep it because of what it had been used for – they considered it 'blood money'. So instead of keeping it they bought a field from a potter, and used the place to bury strangers who didn't have a burial place of their own.

threw [the coins] to the potter at the house of the Lord: when Judas went to the temple to return his traitor's money to the religious leaders, they didn't want anything to do with it. They said his guilty conscience was his problem and so was the money. So he just threw it on the floor in the temple.

Just like in Zechariah, the religious leaders in Jesus' time had done the opposite of their job. Instead of helping the people get closer to God, they were pushing the people further away from God. As a result, God was going to judge all of the people but especially the leaders because their sin was greater.

APPLICATION: Remorse is when we feel bad that we did something because we know that it's wrong. However, instead of confessing it to God and asking his forgiveness we keep just feeling bad. Judas felt 'remorse' because he had betrayed an innocent man, but he still killed himself so his remorse didn't do him any good. Has God helped you to realise that you are a sinner who needs forgiveness? Then tell him about that, ask his forgiveness, trust in what Jesus did on the cross and trust God to keep his promise of forgiveness.

Because of the bad leaders in the time of Zechariah and Jeremiah, as well as in Jesus' time on earth, lots of people in Israel didn't hear God's Word. If you have people who teach you about the Bible, or you read the Bible for yourself, thank God that you are able to know about God's great gift of forgiveness and that you don't have bad leaders stopping you from knowing about the good news.

PRAYER: God, thank you for the Holy Spirit who reminds me that I have disobeyed you, and who shows me through the Bible how I can be forgiven. Please help me to be sorry for my sin and ask you for forgiveness, and trust in Jesus that I am saved. Help me not to be like Judas Iscariot who knew that he had done wrong and felt really bad, but didn't do anything about it. Amen.

PROPHECIES MADE BY JESUS ABOUT HIMSELF

26

JESUS: HE PREDICTED PETER'S DENIALS

MAY
22

PROPHET/DATES: Jesus, about AD 33 on the same evening that he was arrested.

PROPHECY MADE: 'Then Jesus told them, "This very night you will all fall away on account of me, for it is written: 'I will strike the shepherd, and the sheep of the flock will be scattered.' But after I have risen, I will go ahead of you into Galilee." Peter replied, "Even if all fall away on account of you, I never will." "Truly I tell you," Jesus answered, "this very night, before the rooster crows, you will disown me three times." But Peter declared, "Even if I have to die with you, I will never disown you." And all the other disciples said the same' (Matthew 26:31-35 NIV).

THEN AND THERE: Jesus was eating a meal with his disciples (called, 'The Last Supper' because it was the last time they ate together before his death). It must have been a strange and sad time because Jesus knew what he was about to go through. While they were eating dinner he prophesied that he would be betrayed by Judas Iscariot, one of his closest friends. Jesus also predicted that they would all run away because of him. This sounded wrong to Peter, who often said things before he thought about them properly. He was so confident that he would always stand up for Jesus that he said there was no way he would ever pretend not to be Jesus' friend, even if everyone else did.

Can you imagine what Peter must have felt like when he was told he would definitely disown Jesus, and that he would do so three times before the morning! Peter didn't accept what Jesus said – he knew that Jesus was the chosen one from God and did

miracles and possessed incredible wisdom … but even when Jesus made that really detailed prophecy, Peter didn't come close to believing it.

After their meal they sang a hymn then the disciples and Jesus went to a big garden with lots of trees, like a wooded parkland, where Jesus went off on his own to pray. They all had time to think to themselves: what was Judas Iscariot doing? And how or why would Peter possibly pretend not to know Jesus?

PROPHECY FULFILLED: 'Now Peter was sitting out in the courtyard, and a servant girl came to him. "You also were with Jesus of Galilee," she said. But he denied it before them all. "I don't know what you're talking about," he said.

Then he went out to the gateway, where another servant girl saw him and said to the people there, "This fellow was with Jesus of Nazareth." He denied it again, with an oath: "I don't know the man!"

After a little while, those standing there went up to Peter and said, "Surely you are one of them; your accent gives you away." Then he began to call down curses, and he swore to them, "I don't know the man!"

Immediately a rooster crowed. Then Peter remembered the word Jesus had spoken: "Before the rooster crows, you will disown me three times." And he went outside and wept bitterly"'(Matthew 26:69-75 NIV).

SCARLET THREAD: Peter was in real physical danger from an armed mob, whipped up by the religious leaders to be angry and aggressive. These men had just gone out to arrest Jesus while he was praying. They then brought him into Jerusalem. After acting brave at first, Peter followed Jesus at a distance all the way to the courtyard, outside the High Priest's house where Jesus had been taken. Now he had time to think and now he was scared. Peter was surrounded by people who either hated Jesus or had been turned against him. Peter wanted to see what was going on, but if people knew he was a friend of Jesus maybe they'd attack him, or put him in prison too? That's why he lied, pretending not to know Jesus and even getting angry and swearing when people kept telling him that they were sure they'd seen him with Jesus. Then it happened: the rooster crowed and in that moment Peter remembered, and realised he'd done the terrible thing he swore he'd never do. He cried … hard.

The most amazing thing about Peter disowning Jesus is not that he did it – any one of us could be tempted to disown Jesus if we thought someone would kill us for being his friend. The truly wonderful thing is what happened a few days later after Jesus rose from the dead. Jesus forgave Peter for what he did, and even gave Peter great responsibility for sharing the gospel and looking after those who had recently become Christians. Even in the story of Peter disowning Jesus, we see the 'one story' of the Bible: God bringing his people to himself. Even those who have just let him down badly.

APPLICATION: This is another part of the suffering of Jesus: Betrayed by someone who claimed to be his friend but wasn't (Judas Iscariot) and then disowned by someone who really was a good friend (Peter). Jesus suffered so much before he died. We can never say that we've got it hard compared to him. However bad things get we have a Saviour who knows how we feel, who had it even worse than us. That means we can always be comfortable talking to him about our troubles. When we let him down – even if we let him down badly – he is willing to forgive us and welcome us back.

PRAYER: Thank you, God, that you are patient and willing to forgive and use us, just as Peter was forgiven. Thank you that Jesus was not tempted to give up on his mission to die for our sins. Because of all those things, we can be safe with you forever. Amen.

27

JESUS: HE PREDICTED HIS DEATH (THE FIRST TIME)

MAY
22

PROPHET/DATES: Jesus, about AD 33.

PROPHECY MADE: 'From that time on Jesus began to explain to his disciples that he must go to Jerusalem and suffer many things at the hands of the elders, the chief priests and the teachers of the law, and that he must be killed and on the third day be raised to life. Peter took him aside and began to rebuke him. "Never, Lord!" he said. "This shall never happen to you!" Jesus turned and said to Peter, "Get behind me, Satan! You are a stumbling-block to me; you do not have in mind the concerns of God, but merely human concerns"' (Matthew 16:21-23).

THEN AND THERE: Towards the end of Jesus' life on earth, he asked the disciples a question to make them think: 'Who do people say I am?'[14] They told him some people thought he was John the Baptist (who had recently been killed by King Herod), some thought he was the prophet Elijah (who had been taken to heaven in a chariot of fire 850+ years before), some people thought he was the prophet Jeremiah (who had died about 600 years before), and some thought he was one of the other prophets (who had all lived 500-1,000 years before).

Then Jesus asked the disciples who *they* thought he was. We don't know what the other disciples thought, we only know what Peter said: 'You are the Messiah, the Son of the living God'[15]. It seems that after all this time – three years of being a close friend of God-on-earth (Jesus), – Peter finally understood who Jesus was. Phew!

The problem was Peter couldn't handle what Jesus was saying about the terrible things that would be done to him. Maybe he thought Jesus was being negative, talking about how bad things might get if it all went wrong, and at this point Peter thought he'd be brave and make sure it didn't happen, or he just figured Jesus himself could.

---

14. Mark 8:27
15. Matthew 16:16

Peter didn't understand that Jesus' mission on earth was to save people from their sins by his death and resurrection. Telling Jesus it mustn't and wouldn't happen was therefore a terrible thing to say. It was so awful that Jesus felt a temptation from Satan to give up and not allow those things to happen to him; a temptation to say 'No, I'm not going to be tortured and killed; these people don't deserve me to die to save them'. Peter's words sounded like Satan's words – that's why Jesus told Satan to get behind him.

Imagine what Peter must have felt.

PROPHECY FULFILLED: Here are some of the ways that Jesus' prophecy about the religious leaders came true in the space of only a few days.

They got angry with Jesus: 'But when the chief priests and legal experts saw the amazing things he was doing and the children shouting in the temple, "Hosanna to the Son of David!" they were angry [with Jesus]' (Matthew 21:15, CEB).

They said Jesus had no right to say what he was saying: 'Jesus entered the temple courts, and, while he was teaching, the chief priests and the elders of the people came to him. "By what authority are you doing these things?" they asked. "And who gave you this authority?"' (Matthew 21:23).

They tried to make him look bad to the people by tricking him into saying something wrong: 'Then the Pharisees went out and laid plans to trap him in his words' (Matthew 22:15).

They made a plan to arrest Jesus and then kill him: 'When Jesus had finished saying all these things, he said to his disciples, "As you know, the Passover is two days away – and the Son of Man will be handed over to be crucified."

'Then the chief priests and the elders of the people assembled in the palace of the high priest, whose name was Caiaphas, and they schemed to arrest Jesus secretly and kill him. "But not during the festival," they said, "or there may be a riot among the people"' (Matthew 26:1-5).

All these things were just the start of how Jesus would suffer when he was betrayed, arrested, beaten, mocked, tortured, lied about and killed. But these little events show that his enemies kept attacking him, kept coming at him, just like he said they would.

SCARLET THREAD: Jesus spent most of his ministry showing people who he was, giving them proof with his actions (e.g. miracles) and teachings, as well as his perfect behaviour. He spent three years with the twelve disciples doing everything to help them understand that he was God.

Then, once Peter had said he understood who Jesus was, Jesus told them what was going to happen. It wouldn't have made sense before they knew who he was, and now it should have made sense, but it didn't. They failed to understand that all those animal sacrifices in the Old Testament pointed to the ultimate sacrifice of Jesus. When Jesus told them this, although we don't know what the other disciples thought, we know that Peter was horrified.

APPLICATION: Even if we read the Bible a lot, sometimes it's easy to only hear what we want to hear, and to reject what sounds bad. Peter had just said Jesus was God, but then he argued with God! That makes no sense at all but Peter didn't want to hear what Jesus had to say so he rejected it, even though it was for Peter's good (and ours) that Jesus was going to suffer and die.

When you read the Bible, be careful to listen to what God is really saying and not just what you would like him to say. For example, it's hard to hear that we are all sinners and need God's forgiveness, and we want to think that we're OK. But when we accept the truth, then we can have God's free gift of forgiveness because of what Jesus did.

 PRAYER: God, please help me to understand like Peter did, that Jesus is God. And please help me not to be like Peter, who at first rejected what Jesus said because it sounded bad. Please help me to trust everything that Jesus said. Amen.

He must be killed and on the third day be raised to life.

Look, I am coming soon!

They paid me thirty pieces of silver.

Lowly and riding on a donkey.

They will flog him and kill him. On the third day he will rise again.

Strike the shepherd.

After I have risen, I will go ahead of you into Galilee.

28

JESUS: HE PREDICTED HIS DEATH (THE SECOND TIME)

MAY 22

PROPHET/DATES: Jesus, AD 33.

PROPHECY MADE: 'They left that place and passed through Galilee. Jesus did not want anyone to know where they were, because he was teaching his disciples. He said to them, "The Son of Man is going to be delivered into the hands of men. They will kill him, and after three days he will rise." But they did not understand what he meant and were afraid to ask him about it' (Mark 9:30-32).

THEN AND THERE: Hearing that the disciples were 'afraid' to ask Jesus something, reminds us of the first time Jesus predicted his own death and Peter said 'No!' because he didn't want anything bad to happen to Jesus. Jesus responded by saying to Peter, 'Get behind me Satan!' After that happened the disciples probably didn't want to say anything when Jesus next made a horrible-sounding prediction. After all, would you like God treating your words as if they'd come from Satan himself?

This time Peter didn't say 'No'. The disciples just didn't know what Jesus meant! They knew he was talking about himself, because he'd used the name 'Son of Man' about himself before. But dying? And then rising again three days later?? What was *that* about?

'Best keep quiet,' they thought to themselves. I think you and I would probably think the same thing at that point if we didn't understand what Jesus was saying.

 PROPHECY FULFILLED: See how the three parts of the prophecy were fulfilled: '... the Son of Man is delivered into the hands of sinners ...' (Matthew 26:45).

'While he was still speaking, Judas, one of the Twelve, arrived. With him was a large crowd armed with swords and clubs, sent from the chief priests and the elders of the people. Now the betrayer had arranged a signal with them: "The one I kiss is the man; arrest him." Going at once to Jesus, Judas said, "Greetings, Rabbi!" and kissed him. Jesus replied, "Do what you came for, friend." Then the men stepped forward, seized Jesus and arrested him' (Matthew 26:47-50).

'They will kill him ...' (Matthew 17:23).

'When they came to the place called the Skull, they crucified him there ...' (Luke 23:33).

'... and after three days he will rise' (Mark 9:31).

'The angel said to the women, "Do not be afraid, for I know that you are looking for Jesus, who was crucified. He is not here; he has risen, just as he said"' (Matthew 28:5-6).

 SCARLET THREAD: God had been using the prophets for hundreds of years to tell people about the Messiah – the promised one from God who was going to be sent to earth by God. They didn't know when, and they didn't have all the details, but they knew it would happen.

In this prophecy Jesus himself was talking and he could not have been more clear. Notice that Jesus knew details of what was going to happen – frightening details – but he persevered.

 APPLICATION: When Jesus prophesied with such detail about the terrible things that were going to happen, it helps us to realise just how much love he had for us, and for his Father God. He wasn't going through life thinking he might live to be seventy and then was badly surprised when he experienced opposition, persecution, torture and then death. No, he knew what was going to happen and he did it anyway. He didn't want to suffer or to be killed, but what was more important to him was honouring his Father, providing a way for us to be saved, and going to be with his Father again in heaven. For all of those things to happen, he had to go through with the plan.

And he did.

 PRAYER: Thank you, God, that Jesus went through with the plan that means we can be saved from our sins. Thank you that he knew what was going to happen and allowed it to happen to him because we can see that he really loves you and loves us. Amen.

29

JESUS: HE PREDICTED HIS DEATH (THE THIRD TIME)

MAY
22

PROPHET/DATES: Jesus, AD 33.

PROPHECY MADE: 'Jesus took the Twelve aside and told them, "We are going up to Jerusalem, and everything that is written by the prophets about the Son of Man will be fulfilled. He will be handed over to the Gentiles. They will mock him, insult him and spit on him; they will flog him and kill him. On the third day he will rise again"' (Luke 18:31-33).

THEN AND THERE: And here's the response right away: 'The disciples did not understand any of this. Its meaning was hidden from them, and they did not know what he was talking about' (Luke 18:34). Ouch. Here we go … *again!* Because *again*, Jesus' clear prophecy about himself didn't make any sense to the disciples.

After Jesus had risen from the dead he was walking with two people who were very sad. When Jesus asked them why they were sad they were surprised to hear that he hadn't heard the news: that a great and powerful guy called Jesus had died. And that they'd just had some very confusing news, that his tomb was empty.

We can only imagine Jesus' frustrations with his friends as he said, 'How foolish you are, and how slow to believe all that the prophets have spoken! Did not the Messiah have to suffer these things and then enter his glory?'[16]

---

16. Luke 24:25-26

That just goes to show that Jesus wasn't hiding things from people – he was speaking plainly to them, but it was hidden from them. It was far away from what they were expecting so they didn't understand what the prophets had been saying, and what Jesus himself was saying.

Jesus was powerful. Many people loved him, and there were so many good things that they thought he was going to do for the whole country, that they were sure nothing terrible could happen to him. Jesus started out as an adult being a carpenter. He only became full-time in his preaching, teaching and healing when he was thirty years old, and at this point he was only thirty-three. Plenty of time left, they thought, to do wonderful things.

The twelve disciples weren't the only ones who were being slow and failing to understand what they were being told. But it's obvious from what Jesus said that they should have known.

Imagine telling someone that you're going to the movies with your friends, and they then look at you and say, 'What?!' You're going to wonder what their problem is, why they can't understand your clear words to them. That's what it was like for Jesus when he told his disciples for a third time that he was going to be killed.

PROPHECY FULFILLED: In each of the three prophecies that Jesus made to his disciples he mentions slightly different things that will happen to him before he would be killed. In the first he said that he would 'suffer many things' that the religious leaders would do to him. In the second he would be 'delivered' to evil people (a reference to his betrayal by Judas Iscariot). In this one he speaks of being mocked, insulted and spat on.

Here's where it happened. When he was among the Jewish religious leaders 'they spit in his face and struck him with their fists. Others slapped him and said, "Prophesy to us, Messiah. Who hit you?"' (Matthew 26:68) When he had been handed over to Roman soldiers to be killed: 'They stripped him and put a scarlet robe on him, and then twisted together a crown of thorns and set it on his head. They put a staff in his right hand. Then they knelt in front of him and mocked him. "Hail, king of the Jews!" they said. They spat on him, and took the staff and struck him on the head again and again. After they had mocked him, they took off the robe and put his own clothes on him. Then they led him away to crucify him' (Matthew 27:28-31).

SCARLET THREAD: Jesus, the Son of God: Betrayed by his friend. A close friend (Peter) pretends he doesn't even know him. Mocked, insulted, beaten, spat on and lied about by his own people and by Roman soldiers. This all had to happen to Jesus before he was killed, to fulfil prophecy. It's hard to read some of it and perhaps we don't even want to read it because it's so horrible. But they are important parts of the story about what had to happen to Jesus when he came to earth.

APPLICATION: As with the first two, this third prediction of Jesus' suffering gives us good reason to thank God that Jesus went through it willingly. After all, even when Jesus was on earth he was still God as well as a man, and he could have stopped everything, any time he decided to. But he didn't. We should ask God to help us understand the Bible, because without God's help, we can't understand or trust what he's saying. Just like the disciples couldn't understand, even though it should have been clear to them.

PRAYER: God, please help me to understand your Word, the Bible. Help me to understand the bad news about my sin and the good news about the free gift of forgiveness because of what Jesus did. Amen.

(30)

EPILOGUE: JESUS WILL COME AGAIN

Our last prophecy is different. All the other promises in this book that God made have already come true. But there is one, very exciting prophecy, where the fulfilment is in the future. We are still waiting for Jesus Christ the Son of God to return for the second and final time when God makes everything new and all God's people go to be with him forever.

MAY
22

PROPHETS/DATES: Old Testament: Solomon, Micah, Isaiah and Daniel (between 950 and 536 BC) New Testament: Jesus, angels, Peter, Paul (AD 30-68) and John (c. AD 95).

PROPHECIES MADE: Here are four of the many prophecies about Jesus' second coming, made between 550 BC and AD 5:

Prophecy by Daniel, in chapter 7:13−14 (c. 550 BC): 'In my vision at night I looked, and there before me was one like a son of man, coming with the clouds of heaven. He approached the Ancient of Days and was led into his presence. He was given authority, glory and sovereign power; all nations and peoples of every language worshipped him. His dominion is an everlasting dominion that will not pass away, and his kingdom is one that will never be destroyed.'

Most of the Old Testament prophecies about Jesus were about his first coming - that was what the Jews were looking forward to. However, several times in the Old Testament God also talks about the second coming which would not be in humble circumstances like the first one. When Jesus comes again he won't be a baby, and he won't be hidden away in a village in Israel. He will arrive in a spectacular way that everyone can see, and will know that he is the everlasting king.

Prophecy by Jesus, quoted by Matthew in chapter 25:31 (c. AD 33): 'When the Son of Man comes in his glory, and all the angels with him, he will sit on his glorious throne.'

When Jesus came the first time he was worthy of all our praise, but it wasn't obvious if you just looked at him: his appearance, clothes, job, friends, family, and home would not have made you think of the word, 'glorious'. But that will definitely be an obvious and good word to use when Jesus comes again to rule.

Prophecy by Paul: 1 Thessalonians 4:16–18 (c. AD 51): 'For the Lord himself will come down from heaven, with a loud command, with the voice of the archangel and with the trumpet call of God, and the dead in Christ will rise first. After that, we who are still alive and are left will be caught up together with them in the clouds to meet the Lord in the air. And so we will be with the Lord forever. Therefore encourage one another with these words.'

This takes up the theme of Daniel's prophecy, showing that everyone will know about it straight away when Jesus comes again. It will be a glorious occasion, a majestic entrance, and Jesus will take all of his people to be with him just as he promised he would.

Prophecy by Jesus, through John in Revelation 22:12–13, 16 (c. AD 95): 'Look, I am coming soon! My reward is with me, and I will give to each person according to what they have done. I am the Alpha and the Omega, the First and the Last, the Beginning and the End … I, Jesus, have sent my angel to give you this testimony for the churches. I am the Root and the Offspring of David, and the bright Morning Star.'

A day for God is like a thousand years for us, so it has been 2,000 years since Jesus came the first time, and he has not yet returned. But some day he will, and for God it will be soon, but for us … we just don't know, so we want to be ready. It's more important than anything that we have our sins forgiven through confessing them to God, asking him to forgive us and trusting in what Jesus did for us. When we have done that, we will more and more be living for God – we will be ready for Jesus.

SCARLET THREAD & APPLICATION: The whole Bible is about God redeeming (buying back) a people who will be with him forever. All God's warnings involve a punishment of God being separated from us, and all his wonderful promises are focused on God being with us. God's warning is that we need to have our sins forgiven so that we can be with God forever. And if we don't do that, we will be without God forever.

When Jesus comes to 'reward' people, 'according to what they have done' he is talking about those who have repented – who have confessed their sins and asked him to forgive them, trusting in Jesus for forgiveness. If that is true about you, then you didn't just say some things to God and then forget about it, but God is already changing you. When God forgives us he stays with us and starts to make us more like Jesus: hating sin, loving what is good, trying to be more like Jesus, wanting other people to know God too. That's what a Christian looks like, and they are the people who can look forward to Jesus coming again. So when Jesus says again right at the end of the Bible, 'Yes, I am coming soon,' all God's people can say with John: 'Amen. Come Lord Jesus'.

PRAYER: Thank you, God, that every single one of the promises you made about when Jesus first came to earth have come true. Thank you that because of that, we can trust you that all your promises about Jesus' second coming – which hasn't happened yet – will come true. Please help us to be ready for when that happens by trusting you for the forgiveness of our sins and learning to live more and more like our Saviour Jesus. Amen.

10 KEY MEMORY VERSES ABOUT MESSIANIC PROPHECY:

This is how the Israelites were told they could know whether a prophet was real or fake:

'If what a prophet proclaims in the name of the Lord does not take place or come true, that is a message the LORD has not spoken' (Deuteronomy 18:22).

A New Testament writer reminding the people of the importance of the prophets, and how they were also less important than Jesus, because Jesus is God.

'In the past God spoke … through the prophets at many times and in various ways, but in these last days he has spoken to us by his Son, whom he appointed heir of all things, and through whom also he made the universe' (Hebrews 1:1-2).

'… do not believe every spirit, but test the spirits to see whether they are from God, because many false prophets have gone out into the world' (1 John 4:1).

In the next verse John tells us that a key test for prophecy is whether the 'prophet' admits that Jesus is God and came to earth as a real man.

Jesus encouraged his disciples to persevere when they were telling people about him, knowing that they would be persecuted, just as the prophets were persecuted: 'Rejoice and be glad, because great is your reward in heaven, for in the same way they persecuted the prophets who were before you' (Matthew 5:12).

To people who accused him of throwing away the Old Testament, Jesus said, 'Do not think that I have come to abolish the Law or the Prophets; I have not come to abolish them but to fulfill them' (Matthew 5:17).

How important is Old Testament prophecy?

'We also have the prophetic message as something completely reliable, and you will do well to pay attention to it, as to a light shining in a dark place, until the day dawns and the morning star rises in your hearts' (2 Peter 1:19).

Where does prophecy come from?

Peter said, 'For prophecy never had its origin in the human will, but prophets, though human, spoke from God as they were carried along by the Holy Spirit' (2 Peter 1:21).

The prophets didn't just give predictions, they were communicating what God was like and how he felt about his people.

'Jesus replied, "Love the Lord your God with all your heart and with all your soul and with all your mind"... [and] ... "Love your neighbour as yourself. All the Law and the Prophets hang on these two commandments"'(Matthew 22:37-40).

'Philip found Nathanael and told him, "We have found the one Moses wrote about in the Law, and about whom the prophets also wrote—Jesus of Nazareth, the son of Joseph"' (John 1:45).

God is in charge and his Word is true:

'... this is how God fulfilled what he had foretold through all the prophets, saying that his Messiah would suffer. Repent, then, and turn to God, so that your sins may be wiped out ...' (Acts 3:18-19).

CHARACTER PROFILES

MOSES

ISAIAH

JONAH

DAVID

MOSES

- What did he do? He spent his first forty years in Egypt living in the palace, even though he was a Hebrew, his next forty years in exile when he ran away after killing an Egyptian slave master, and his last forty years leading the Hebrews through the desert. He died just before they entered the promised land.
- What did he write? Most likely Genesis, Leviticus, Numbers, Deuteronomy and parts of Exodus.
- Where is his story? Mainly in the book of Exodus.

KING DAVID

- What did he do? From humble beginnings as the youngest son of a sheep-herding family, David rose to fame after killing the Philistine giant Goliath, then became one of the most successful soldiers in Israelite history, becoming the second King of Israel and reigning for forty years.
- What did he write? Many of the psalms.
- Where is his story? He comes on the scene in 1 Samuel 16 and is the main character from there until the end of 2 Samuel. He dies in 1 Kings 2.

ASAPH

- What did he do? He was probably one of the three Levites whom King David put in charge of the singing in the temple.
- What did he write? Psalm 50 and 73-83.
- Where is his story? Nowhere that we know of! He had an important role in Israel, but his story is not a big part of the story of God's people.

NATHAN

- What did he do? He was a prophet during the reign of King David who confronted the king about his son after his adultery with Bathsheba followed by the murder of her husband Uriah.
- What did he write? None of the books of the Bible are by him.
- Where is his story? He is famous for that one incident with King David and Bathsheba – we don't know anything else about him.

JONAH

- What did he do? God sent him to be a missionary to the city of Nineveh – a wicked place that persecuted Israel. Jonah ran away from God's command and was swallowed by a big fish. Ultimately he did obey God, and when the Ninevites repented and God saved them, Jonah got angry.
- What did he write? We don't know for certain that he wrote anything, although he may have contributed to the book of Jonah.
- Where is his story? The book of Jonah in the Bible.

ISAIAH

- What did he do? He spent about twenty-five years prophesying in the northern country of Israel, about the judgment that was coming for Israel, but also about God restoring them.
- What did he write? The book of Isaiah.
- Where is his story? He doesn't write about himself in his prophecy and we don't have his life story anywhere else, but we know he was married and had at least two sons.

MICAH

- What did he do? He was a prophet from southern Judah, telling the people in the southern kingdom about the terrible defeat of the northern kingdom and how the same was going to happen to them if they didn't turn back to God. He also spoke about God saving his people.
- What did he write? The book of Micah.
- Where is his story? Another semi-anonymous prophet who enters the Bible story purely because God gave him an important message, and not because anything very interesting happened to him apart from that massive privilege!

HOSEA

- What did he do? He wrote down prophecies from God of judgment and deliverance.
- What did he write? The only writings we have are in the book with his name.
- Where is his story? The book of Hosea contains both his prophecies and also his story.

DANIEL

- What did he do? Daniel was the only prophet we know of who lived before the exile, during all the exile in Babylon, and then came back after the exile. He refused to stop praying to God and was thrown into a den of lions because of it, but God saved him and he spent his time in Babylon in a high government position.
- What did he write? The book of Daniel.
- Where is his story? The book of Daniel.

JEREMIAH

- What did he do? He prophesied to kings and rulers during the last days of Judah, warning them to repent. Then, after their defeat by Babylon, warning people not to run away to Egypt in disobedience to God. Most people ignored him completely, and a lot of those who didn't ignore him, persecuted him.
- What did he write? Other than his own book of Jeremiah, he also wrote the book of Lamentations.
- Where is his story? We read a lot of his story between the prophecies written down in his book.

ZECHARIAH

- What did he do? Born while Judah was in exile in Babylon, Zechariah was a priest who returned to his homeland when the exile was over. Most likely eventually becoming high priest, some time after he had finished prophesying.
- What did he write? The book of Zechariah.
- Where is his story? Mentioned in the books of Nehemiah and Ezra, most of what we know about Zechariah is from his own book of prophecy.

Prophecies about Jesus' Birth

2 Samuel 7:12-16
Isaiah 7:14-16
Micah 5:2
Hosea 11:1
Jeremiah 31:15

Prophecies about Jesus' Death

Psalm 34:19-20; Exodus 12:46
Psalm 22:1-3
Psalm 22:6-8
Psalm 22:16-18
Zechariah 13:7
Matthew 26:31-35
Matthew 16:21-23
Matthew 9:30-32
Luke 18:31-33

Prophecies about Jesus' Resurrection

Psalm 16:9-10
Luke 18:31-33

Prophecies about Jesus' Betrayal and Rejection

Matthew 26:31-35
Zechariah 11:12-13
Zechariah 13:7
Psalm 118:22-24
Psalm 69:4
Psalm 22:6-8
Psalm 69:8
Psalm 41:7-9

Prophecies about What Jesus Did

Isaiah 35:3-6
Psalm 78:2
Genesis 3:15

Prophecies about Who Jesus Is

Daniel 7:13-14
Zechariah 9:9
Isaiah 42:1-4
2 Samuel 7:12-16
Psalm 110:4
Deuteronomy 18:18-19

Page 37 Answers: Psalm 41; Psalm 78; Psalm 22; Psalm 34; Psalm 110
Page 53 Answers:
The stone the builders rejected - A prophecy of how Jesus Christ would be rejected by the leaders.
The sign of the prophet Jonah - A prophecy of how Jesus Christ would be three days in the tomb.
Your throne will be established forever - A prophecy of how Jesus Christ would rise from the dead and ascend into heaven, one day returning in victory.
They divide my clothes among them - A prophecy of how the soldiers would divide Jesus' clothes between them at his death.
You will not abandon me to the realm of the dead - A prophecy about Jesus Christ's resurrection.
Page 81 Answers
- Lowly and riding on a donkey.
- They paid me thirty pieces of silver.
- Strike the shepherd.
- He must be killed and on the third day be raised to life.
- They will flog him and kill him. On the third day he will rise again
- After I have risen, I will go ahead of you into Galilee.
- Look, I am coming soon!

ACKNOWLEDGEMENTS

Having children who ask questions is a huge blessing, especially when they keep asking as they get older and the questions become ever more searching. My overwhelming desire for them to know and love God's Word, and through that to know and love God himself drove most of the thought, prayer and writing that went into this book. So, thank you Jude and Alice.

Thank you to Mam and Dad, who modelled that desire for me when I was a child, and who haven't changed in that regard one bit.

Thank you to my friends and spiritual family at FBC of Grand Cayman, who have been home since we got off the plane twelve years ago; thank you for your encouragements.

PAUL REYNOLDS

ENDORSEMENTS

We want our children, our grandchildren, and all children, to catch the vision of God's purposes in the world. We want them to long for His Kingdom to come, to seek first the Kingdom and His righteousness. And there is no better way to fuel a passion for the Kingdom, than to have a clear grasp of God's faithfulness in keeping his promises. This beautifully designed book outlines thirty of God's promises, joining each of them up with their Gospel fulfilment in Christ. A marvellous resource for children, parents, and Bible teachers.

Dr Sharon James
Social Policy Analyst, The Christian Institute

This book is an excellent way to introduce young people to the topic of prophecy in Scripture. In clear, easy to understand explanations, Paul Reynolds points out how Scripture prepared the world for Christ's coming and then recorded Christ's fulfillment of those predictions. This book gives practical applications from Scripture and is ideal for personal or family devotions.

Heather LeFebvre
Author of *The History of Christmas*, Blogger @
Blackberry Rambles

Paul Reynolds systematically shows how the prophecies about Jesus, and by Jesus, concerning his life, death and resurrection absolutely come true in detail. He also helpfully points out what the prophecies would have meant in their original context. This would make excellent Bible detective work for a family prayers setting. The structured pattern and the attractive illustrations make it very user friendly and the applications and prayers are challenging and relevant.

Ann Benton

Author of *Aren't They Lovely When They're Asleep*

With your children, grandchildren etc, I'd recommend your reading together a chapter a day to learn, reflect and pray your way through this helpful guide to some of the Bible's wonderful prophecies that unmistakably point to the coming of the Lord Jesus. You won't be disappointed!

Dr Steve Brady
Senior Minister, First Baptist Church, Grand Cayman,
& President, Moorlands College, Christchurch, U.K.

MEET THE AUTHOR

PAUL REYNOLDS is a member at First Baptist Church of Grand Cayman. He and his wife Rachael have two children: Jude and Alice. Paul enjoys photography, travel, sports and writing.

FROM THE AUTHOR

As with '66 Books One Story', my main hope is that this book will help connect people with what the Bible is saying so that they become connected with God.

Amid all the complexities and 'tough bits' of the Bible, God has been doing some seriously straightforward work that we can easily miss. For example, Jesus wasn't a counter-intuitive shock to the system who was understandably rejected. Rather, his life was by far the most predictable and predicted series of events in human history, and the rejection of him by so many people 2,000 years ago is the same as the rejection of him now: people don't want to owe everything to God, and they want to be god of their own world. The more we can see the flow of what God is saying throughout Scripture, the more confidence we can have in God's Word and the more we may grow to love Him for all that he has been doing and encourage others to do the same.

Paul Reynolds

MEET THE ARTIST

SARAH DOUGLAS graduated from Loughborough University with a degree in Illustration after focusing her studies on children's illustration and book design. Shortly after, she had the opportunity to illustrate her first book and has since been involved in an array of work including surface pattern design, greetings card design and now freelancing as a book illustrator.

Sarah grew up in North Wales and was drawn to illustration as she enjoyed the variety of skills and projects it encompassed. She now resides in Bristol with her husband Phil and enjoys spending her weekends exploring the city, juggling freelance and personal projects and catching up with friends.

CHRISTIAN FOCUS PUBLICATIONS

Christian Focus Publications publishes books for adults and children under its four main imprints: Christian Focus, CF4K, Mentor and Christian Heritage. Our books reflect our conviction that God's Word is reliable and Jesus is the way to know him, and live for ever with him. Our children's list includes a Sunday School curriculum that covers pre-school to early teens, and puzzle and activity books. We also publish personal and family devotional titles, biographies and inspirational stories that children will love. If you are looking for quality Bible teaching for children, then we have an excellent range of Bible stories and age-specific theological books. From pre-school board books to teenage apologetics, we have it covered!

CF4•K
Because you're never
too young to know Jesus

CHRISTIAN FOCUS PUBLICATIONS
Christian   Christian   CF4K   Mentor
Focus   Heritage